Chefman Digital Air Fryer Oven Cookbook

1000-Day Quick & Simple Flavorful Recipes to Air Fry, Roast, Broil, Bake, Bagel, Toast, Dehydrate and Reheat Your Favorite Gourmet Meals.

Sharon Watson

TABLE OF CONTENTS

INTRODUCTION

Congratulations; your decision to buy this Air Fryer cookbook shows that you have good judgment. This book has delectable Air Fryer recipes that are guaranteed to impress everyone. You can read about all the different ways to cook delicious foods with an air fryer on the pages that follow. Not only will these foods taste fantastic, but they will also be healthier for you overall and have fewer calories. The recipes are easy to understand, follow, and make. You will really love how quick and simple utilizing an air fryer makes cooking. You'll find that the recipes in this book have a flavor that is enticing, crisp, and fresh. You can prepare delicious meals when you cook using an air fryer. With the help of these cooking gadgets, you can cook foods that would traditionally be deep-fried while using up to 80% less oil, enhancing the nutritional value of the finished product. Superheated air is used to cook the meal, and the cooking chamber features a fan that moves the air around like one would in a convection oven. In addition to being able to prepare foods that you would ordinarily deep fry, you can create other meals faster than it would take in the oven. Roast pork, ham, lamb chops, hamburgers, scrambled eggs, quiche, baked apples, cakes, pies, and cookies should all be made. By using a few specialized tools, you can prepare almost anything that can be cooked in your oven in a fraction of the time. Fried chicken, or any of your other favorite dishes, come out crispy and moist, so you won't need a napkin to clean the grease off your fingers after eating it.

Thanks to your Air Fryer, you'll be able to eat less fat while still savoring your favorite meals, such french fries, country fried steak, and a range of delectable fish dishes. You can also make a wide range of different dinners, including roast beef, a rack of lamb, pulled pork, lobster tails, and a lot of other big dish feasts. You can then proceed to create some delicious appetizers like stuffed mushrooms, potato skins, and onion rings once you have finished cooking those. For your enjoyment, I've also included a number of delectable desserts that can all be made in an air fryer, including chocolate cake, apple pie, cookies, and a few others.

In this book, the topic is not finished. It's uncommon to find frozen foods with instructions on how to use an air fryer, and those that do are few and far between. I've provided easy-to-follow instructions that can be used to prepare a number of your favorite frozen foods. You'll find that your previously frozen food is now delicious, crispy, and uses much less oil. You can prepare a range of items, such as frozen chicken nuggets, poppers, pizza rolls, hamburgers, chicken breasts, and more, in a fraction of the time it takes to prepare them using conventional methods.

An air fryer allows you to cook in much less time and may be used to cook almost any cuisine. Your meals won't be made using traditional recipes because they have higher cholesterol and calorie counts. This book will guide you through the process of cooking delicious meals in an Air Fryer, which is a win-win situation. There are recipes provided for breakfast, lunch, and dinner. There are also delectable recipes available for starters, snacks, sides, and sweet desserts. Read on to find out everything you need to know about using an air fryer to make delicious meals with more flavor and less grease than you would with conventional frying techniques.

CHAPTER 1: CHEFMAN AIR FRYER FOR BEGINNERS

"Rapid air Technology," the technology used in air fryers, is in charge of distributing the heat through the use of a fan that rotates very quickly. Unless the oven in question is a convection oven, fans that continuously circulate the heat are not normally incorporated in ovens. Food is placed in a removable basket and cooked in an air fryer by hot air that circulates all around the basket. One of the most well-liked items to cook in an air fryer is frequently listed as french fries. These delectable morsels are frequently deep-fried at a high temperature after spending some time submerged in a vat of oil. A sizable percentage of the oil is kept by the potatoes, which is then used for cooking. It is well known that oil does not always provide health benefits for people. Certain oils contribute to the buildup of plaque in our blood vessels and add superfluous fat to our bodies. How could you possibly make a mistake if the food tastes just as excellent, if not better, after using less oil? I use my air fryer almost weekly when I make sweet potato fries. The only steps in this recipe are to peel the potato, cut it into thick strips, sprinkle it with a tablespoon of olive oil and some spices, and then air fry it. They can be prepared and cooked in just ten minutes, but they turn out crispy on the outside and tender on the inside. It only takes about that time, and they are far superior to any fries that are fried in hot oil.

What Can You Cook In Your Air Fryer?

Anything that you would typically deep fry can be prepared, but there are other options as well. An air fryer can perfectly cook fries, chicken nuggets, fried fish, fried chicken, and all of these other unhealthy foods, making them more safer to eat. However, using an air fryer for that purpose is not the only option. My homemade French toast or scrambled eggs are usually what I have for breakfast. If I wanted, I could make some empanadas or Chinese dumplings for lunch. You can quickly create meals like meatloaf, pork chops, salmon, country-style fried steak, and barbecue chicken in the air fryer. Certain meals, including soup or stew, can be cooked in an air fryer as long as they don't contain any liquid. An air fryer can be used to make sweet delights like cake, hand pies, and other pastries in addition to frying food.

The air fryer basket has slots or perforations all around it to allow air to flow freely through it. I can't use that basket for some of the items I prepare in my air fryer because they would pour out all over the place if I did. To solve this issue, I use ceramic ramekins, a tiny metal bowl with a flat bottom, or a small metal cake pan with a diameter between 6 and 4 inches to cook things like scrambled eggs. Additionally, some air fryers available on the market include a part similar to this that may be inserted into the basket. This offers a wide range of fresh options for the dishes that can be cooked in an air fryer.

Healthier Food With Your Air Fryer?

In addition to circulating hot air around the food in the air fryer, the fan also expels oil droplets and initiates the Mallard Effect, a chemical reaction. In addition to making the meal darker and crispier than it was before, this reaction gives the food some flavor. Foods that are fried in an air fryer have a lot less fat but either the same taste or a better taste. The quantity of fat in roasted or baked chicken is comparable to that in fried chicken that has been made in an air fryer. Not only do meals have less fat, but they also contain fewer calories. When food is fried, a chemical is produced on it that is transferred to the food that we eat. The chemical in concern is called acrylamide, and it is thought to be carcinogenic (causes cancer). According to the results of a study that was conducted, when food was prepared using an air fryer, the acrylamide content was found to be reduced by a factor of 90. I have a rocky relationship with fried foods. I eat them, which directly causes me to experience painful heartburn and cramps in my stomach. Eating french fries or other fried foods cooked in an air fryer had no negative consequences on me. My own weight loss has made it clear that meals made in an air fryer are healthier for me than those made in other ways.

Benefits of Your Air Fryer

The advantages of owning an air fryer, in my opinion, much outweigh any potential disadvantages. I regularly use mine, and even though I have a gas stove, I've noticed a drop in the price of gas while also not noticing a noticeable increase in the price of electricity. That is without a doubt a point in my favor, in my opinion.

Benefits

- The usage of oil in cooking has been drastically cut back, which results in healthier food. Despite this, everything that should be brown and crispy turns out to be when it should.
- The food will cook more quickly. In contrast to a stovetop or oven, an air fryer does not allow heat to escape while it is in use. Because the food is kept in the air fryer and continually circulated, the process of cooking or reheating it takes significantly less time.
- The air fryer is more time and energy saving. Because the heat is contained within the appliance rather than escaping through vents, the food is cooked more quickly and effectively while requiring a lower amount of electricity. When the weather outside is warm, the last thing I want to do is turn on the oven and make the house even hotter. But this is not the case with an air fryer. The heat that is generated within the air fryer is retained within the device.
- Because of its adaptability, it may be used to prepare a wide variety of dishes, ranging from appetizers to sweets.
- The vast majority of models are compact and may be easily stashed away in a cabinet or on a kitchen counter. If you don't like things sitting on your countertops, this could be considered a disadvantage.
- They are rather simple to clean, and the majority of their components, such as the basket and the section that supports the basket, can be cleaned in a dishwasher.
- Foods like chicken tenders and nuggets, fish sticks, and frozen fries can be cooked in a matter of minutes when they are heated from the freezer and then placed in an oven at a higher temperature than they would normally be cooked at.

Types of Air Fryers

Today's market offers three different kinds of air fryers, including:

- Cooking using a halogen oven requires the use of a halogen light bulb. These typically have a see-through glass cover that allows you to monitor the entire cooking process without having to open the air fryer.
- Dynamic: Equipped with a paddle that rotates the food while it is being cooked, eliminating the need to turn it over halfway through the process. This works out great for producing french fries, but it is not nearly as useful for preparing other things. If I were to put some of my empanadas or dumplings in one of these, and then rotate it with the paddle, the stuffing would

come out all over the place.

- The term "Static Air" refers to a situation in which all external conditions remain unchanged, with the exception of the air within the unit, which is warmed by coil elements and blown around by a fan. When purchasing an air fryer, the vast majority of consumers go with this model.

For air fryers, a variety of capacities are offered. My basket has a diameter of roughly 6 inches and can cook up to 1.8 pounds of food at once. There are various types that can simultaneously cook 1.5 to 2.5 pounds of food.

Accessories

Some air fryers feature the following accessories:

- Steamer
- Grill pan
- Baking dish
- Silicone pan or cups
- Racks that go inside the basket
- Rubber ended tongs that do not scratch

Purchasing rubber-ended tongs, silicone cups or pans, a steamer, and a baking dish are all necessary. Additionally, investing in silicone cups or a pan is worthwhile. The surface of the basket will be damaged if you use a fork to remove food from it, which will make it easier for food and other objects to attach to the basket in the future.

I was lucky to locate a couple tiny round layer cake pans at the local thrift shop. Just enough room is left for the rubber-tipped tongs to be inserted and used to remove the object from the air fryer when using the one with a six-inch diameter, which fits completely inside the appliance. The 4-inch ramekin is perfect for this use and can be used to prepare omelets for one serving.

Expert Tips

Making the most of your air fryer is easy with the help of the following advice:

- It is recommended that you let your air fryer to reach the desired temperature before adding any food. Even though not all of the recipes ask for it, I still do this step. I first preheat the fryer to the temperature specified in the recipe, then add the food and let it cook for one to four minutes. I have to preheat for a longer period of time whenever I put in a larger item. If I were cooking a couple of chicken breasts, I would prepare for four minutes, but if I were cooking a few fries, I would only preheat for one or two minutes. If the food that is going to be cooked in the air fryer is going to be frozen, then I let it preheat for a little bit longer. When I prepare my own chicken nuggets, I give them a two-minute head start in the oven. I always preheat the oven for four minutes before cooking frozen chicken nuggets.
- There are many recipes that call for the food to be coated with cooking spray; therefore, you should ensure that you have a range of sprays available, including those tasting like butter and those made with olive oil or canola oil. In the kitchen, I find that a pump spray bottle that also accommodates different oils, in addition to olive oil, is the most convenient option.
- It is essential, when breading items to be air fried, to first dredge them in flour and then press the breadcrumbs into the meat. After this, the items can be air fried. If you don't position the breadcrumbs correctly, the powerful fan will blow them away and you'll have to start over.
- The smoking of fatty items like as bacon or ham can be prevented by placing a tablespoon or

so of water in the drawer that holds the basket.

- Use toothpicks to keep the tops of the sandwiches in place, and then trim the sandwiches so that they end just above the food they are holding. The fan of an air fryer is incredibly powerful, and as a result, it frequently causes the top bread to separate from a sandwich as it is cooking.
- Never pack too much into the basket since it will prevent the food from cooking evenly. Everything needs to be in a single layer and there should be no overlap.
- The majority of foods cooked in an air fryer should be flipped over halfway through the stipulated time for cooking. This ensures that the food cooks at a uniform rate. Obviously, there are going to be some things that you won't be able to accomplish this with.
- Always use a thermometer with instant reading capabilities to ensure that meat and other foods that could potentially cause food poisoning are cooked thoroughly before consuming them. If it does not satisfy the standards for that food, put it back in the oven for a little longer (maybe one or two minutes more), check it again, and then put it back in the oven. When cooking frozen items, this is a very important step to take.
- If you put a cake pan or metal dish that is low in weight in your air fryer, you need not be bothered if it produces a lot of noise. You will hear it clanging around in there, especially if there isn't much else in there, because the fan is going to push it around and move it around. In order to prepare scrambled eggs, you need to air fry the butter in a pan while you are preheating the air fryer. This will cause the air fryer to make clanging noises for the entire two minutes that it is preheating. After the eggs have been placed within, the basket will get weighted down, and it will no longer move around or make any noise.

Start utilizing your air fryer for some cooking right now. Never forget to watch what you're cooking as you go because different air fryers may cook at quite different temperatures and timeframes. Start with breakfast before moving on to other meals, such as snacks, desserts, and prepared foods.

CHAPTER 2: BREAKFAST RECIPES

Harvest Granola

Prep: 10 Minutes | **Cook Time:** 30 Minutes | **Makes:** 2 Servings

Ingredients:

- 1 cup sliced almonds
- ½ cup rolled oats
- ¼ cup pumpkin seeds
- A pinch of sea salt
- 2 teaspoons Canola Oil
- ¼ cup maple syrup
- 1 cup Dried Cranberries

Side Servings:

- 2 cups milk (personal preference)

Directions:

1. In a large bowl, combine all the listed ingredients except for the milk.
2. Place a cake pan inside the air fryer basket and line it with parchment paper.
3. Transfer the mixture from the bowl into the lined cake pan.
4. Insert the basket into the air fryer unit.
5. Set the temperature to 220 degrees F or 104 degrees C and cook for 30 minutes, stirring the ingredients halfway through.
6. Once the ingredients are roasted to perfection, serve with a glass of milk. Enjoy!

Nutrition Facts:

- Servings: 2
- Calories per serving: 742
- Total Fat: 42.7g (55% Daily Value)
- Total Carbohydrate: 70.5g (26% Daily Value)
- Protein: 25g

Homemade Granola

Prep: 12 Minutes | **Cook Time:** 33 Minutes | **Makes:** 3 Servings

Main Ingredients:

- 2 cups whole rolled oats
- ¼ cup chopped walnuts
- ¼ cup coconut flakes (optional)
- 1 teaspoon cinnamon
- Pinch of sea salt
- 2 tablespoons melted coconut oil

Other Ingredients:

- 2 tablespoons peanut butter
- 1/3 cup chopped fresh strawberries
- 4 cups of milk (as needed)

Directions:

1. In a medium-sized bowl, combine all the main ingredients.
2. Place a cake pan inside the air fryer basket and line it with round parchment paper.
3. Transfer the mixture from the bowl into the prepared cake pan.
4. Set the air fryer temperature to 220 degrees F (104 degrees C) and cook for 33 minutes. Remember to stir the ingredients halfway through.
5. Once done, add the milk, peanut butter, and chopped strawberries.
6. Serve and enjoy!

Nutrition Facts:

- Servings: 3
- Calories per serving: 499
- Total Fat: 31.3g (40% Daily Value)
- Total Carbohydrate: 40g (15% Daily Value)
- Protein: 19.7g

Chess Filled Bread for Breakfast

Preparation Time: 20 Minutes | **Cook Time:** 20 Minutes | **Servings:** 2

Ingredients:

- ½ pound top round, cooked and thinly sliced
- ½ white onion, caramelized
- 1 cup shredded Parmesan cheese
- Salt and pepper, to taste
- 1 round crusty loaf of bread

Directions:

1. In a bowl, combine the caramelized onions, half of the shredded Parmesan cheese, and the thinly sliced cooked top round.
2. Mix the ingredients thoroughly and season with salt and pepper to your preference.
3. Slice off the top of the crusty loaf of bread, making sure not to cut all the way through.
4. Hollow out the bread loaf to create a cavity.
5. Fill the bread with the mixture from the bowl, and top it with the remaining Parmesan cheese.
6. Place the stuffed bread inside a basket lined with parchment paper.
7. Bake at 350 degrees F (176 degrees C) for 20 minutes.
8. Once done, serve and savor.

Nutrition Facts:

- Servings: 2
- Calories per serving: 586
- Total Fat: 29.7g (38% Daily Value)
- Total Carbohydrate: 17.6g (6% Daily Value)
- Protein: 63.5g

Breakfast Delicious Donuts

Preparation Time: 15 Minutes | **Cook Time:** 5 Minutes | **Makes:** 4 Servings

Ingredients:

- 1 packet of yeast
- 1 cup of full-fat milk
- 2 small organic eggs
- ¼ teaspoon cinnamon
- 2 tablespoons unsalted butter
- 2 cups of flour
- ¼ teaspoon nutmeg
- ½ cup sugar
- Pinch of sea salt

Directions:

1. In a mixing bowl, combine salt, cinnamon, nutmeg, butter, sugar, milk, and yeast.
2. Start the mixer and gradually add the flour to the bowl.
3. While the mixer is running, crack the eggs into it.
4. Once a smooth dough forms, transfer it to a clean work surface. Knead the dough and place it on a large sheet of buttered paper.
5. Roll out the dough and cut it into doughnut shapes using a cutter. Arrange them on the air fryer basket greased with oil.
6. Set the air fryer timer to 5 minutes at 400 degrees F (204 degrees C). Once done, serve.

Nutrition Facts:

- Servings: 4
- Calories per serving: 399
- Total Fat: 4.5g (6% Daily Value)
- Total Carbohydrate: 78.8g (29% Daily Value)
- Protein: 11.2g

Pumpkin Muffins

Preparation Time: 20 Minutes | **Cook Time:** 18 Minutes | **Makes:** 4 Servings

Ingredients:

- 2 cups of all-purpose flour
- 1 teaspoon baking soda
- ½ teaspoon baking powder
- 1 teaspoon ground cinnamon
- ½ teaspoon grated ground nutmeg
- 3 large eggs
- A pinch of salt
- ½ cup dark brown sugar
- 1 cup pumpkin puree
- 1/4 cup almond milk

Directions:

1. Line muffin cups in 4 ramekins and set them aside for later use.
2. In a bowl, combine baking powder, baking soda, grated nutmeg, dark brown sugar, and ground cinnamon. Gradually add in the flour while mixing.
3. In another bowl, whisk the eggs and then add almond milk, mixing thoroughly. Incorporate this mixture into the flour mixture. Once the batter is well-blended, fold in the pumpkin puree.
4. Fill the ramekins with the prepared batter.
5. Place the ramekins into the air fryer baskets and insert them into the air fryer. Set the timer to 350 degrees F (176 degrees C) for 16-18 minutes.
6. Remember to rotate the ramekins after 7 minutes of cooking. Once the muffins are done, serve them for a delightful breakfast.

Nutrition Facts:

- Servings: 4
- Calories per serving: 409
- Total Fat: 8.2g (11% Daily Value)
- Total Carbohydrate: 72.5g (26% Daily Value)
- Protein: 12.3g

Chocolate Glazed Donuts

Prep: 10 Minutes | **Cook Time:** 8 Minutes | **Makes:** 2 Servings

Ingredients:

- 1 large can of biscuits
- 2 tablespoons of butter
- 2 teaspoons of cinnamon
- 1/4 cup of brown sugar

Ingredients for Glaze:

- ½ cup of powdered sugar
- 1 teaspoon of vanilla extract
- 16 tablespoons of milk
- 10 tablespoons of cocoa powder
- 4 tablespoons of coconut oil

Directions:

1. Begin by preparing the glaze. In a bowl, combine all the ingredients for the glaze and set it aside for later use.
2. Preheat the air fryer to 350 degrees F or 176 degrees C for a few minutes.
3. Roll out the biscuit dough and cut it into the shape of doughnuts.
4. Whisk together the butter, sugar, and cinnamon, then brush this mixture over the doughnuts.
5. Place the doughnuts in the air fryer basket lined with parchment paper.
6. Set the timer for 6-8 minutes, making sure to flip the doughnuts halfway through the cooking time.
7. Once done, serve the doughnuts with the prepared glaze drizzled on top.

Nutrition Facts:

- Servings: 2
- Calories per serving: 758
- Total Fat: 49.5g (63% Daily Value)
- Total Carbohydrate: 84.3g (31% Daily Value)
- Protein: 10.9g

Banana Bread

Preparation Time: 22 Minutes | **Cook Time:** 40 Minutes | **Makes:** 4 Servings

Ingredients:

- 2 cups of all-purpose flour
- 1-1/4 teaspoon baking powder
- A pinch of salt
- 4 large bananas, peeled and ripe
- 1 cup brown sugar
- 4 large eggs
- 2 tablespoons of Greek yogurt
- 4 tablespoons of peanut butter
- 1 teaspoon vanilla extract
- ½ cup mini chocolate chips (optional)

Directions:

1. Start by preheating the air fryer to 350 degrees F (176 degrees C) for a few minutes. Line a cake pan with parchment paper.
2. In a bowl, combine the all-purpose flour, baking powder, a pinch of salt, and brown sugar.
3. In a separate bowl, whisk the eggs, and then add peanut butter, Greek yogurt, and vanilla extract. Mix until well combined. Next, incorporate the flour mixture into the egg mixture and mix thoroughly.
4. Fold in the mashed bananas and, if desired, the mini chocolate chips into the batter. Ensure everything is evenly distributed.
5. Pour the prepared batter into the cake pan.
6. Place the cake pan in the air fryer basket and cook at 310 degrees F (154 degrees C) for 40 minutes.
7. Once done, allow it to cool before slicing and serving.

Nutrition Facts:

- Servings: 4
- Calories per serving: 706
- Total Fat: 15.7g (20% Daily Value)
- Total Carbohydrate: 122.3g (44% Daily Value)
- Protein: 23.4g

Avocado Toast

Prep: 12 Minutes | **Cook Time:** 10 Minutes | **Makes:** 2 Servings

Ingredients:

- 2 ripe avocados
- 1 tablespoon of lemon juice
- Salt, to taste
- Pinch of paprika
- 4 slices of grain bread
- 2 tablespoons of butter
- ½ cup of crumbled feta cheese
- 2 teaspoons of balsamic vinegar

Directions:

1. In a bowl, mash the pitted avocados and mix them with lemon juice, a pinch of paprika, and salt.
2. Spread butter on one side of each bread slice.
3. Place the bread slices with the buttered side facing up inside a basket lined with parchment paper.
4. Set the air fryer temperature to 350 degrees F (176 degrees C) and cook for 10 minutes, flipping the bread halfway through for even toasting.
5. Once the bread is perfectly toasted, spread the avocado mash generously on each slice.
6. Sprinkle crumbled feta cheese over the avocado mash.
7. Finish by drizzling balsamic vinegar over the top.
8. Serve and enjoy!

Nutrition Facts:

- Servings: 2
- Calories per serving: 752
- Total Fat: 61g (78% Daily Value)
- Total Carbohydrate: 41.7g (15% Daily Value)
- Protein: 16.3g

Zucchini Corn Fritters

Preparation Time: 40 Minutes | **Cook Time:** 12 Minutes | **Makes:** 2 Servings

Ingredients:

- 2 medium zucchinis, peeled
- 1 cup corn kernels
- ½ potatoes, cooked
- 6 teaspoons chickpea flour
- 1 garlic clove, minced
- 2 tablespoons olive oil
- 1/3 cup shredded parmesan cheese
- Salt and black pepper, to taste
- Oil spray for greasing

Directions:

1. Begin by grating the peeled and washed zucchinis using a grater. Place them in a bowl and add salt. Allow them to sit for 20 minutes, then drain the excess liquid by squeezing.
2. Mix in the rest of the ingredients listed, forming roughly shaped patties.
3. Grease a basket with oil spray and arrange the patties inside in batches.
4. Cook them for 12 minutes at 375 degrees F (190 degrees C), remembering to flip them halfway through.
5. Once cooked, serve and savor the flavors.

Nutrition Facts:

- Servings: 2
- Calories per serving: 488
- Total Fat: 25.6g (33% Daily Value)
- Total Carbohydrate: 49.8g (18% Daily Value)
- Protein: (Value not provided, please add it for completeness)

Bacon Crescent Rolls

Preparation Time: 10 Minutes | **Cook Time:** 12 Minutes | **Makes:** 2 Servings

Ingredients:

- 6 ounces crescent rolls
- 6 bacon strips, cooked and crumbled
- ½ teaspoon onion powder

Directions:

1. Begin by preheating the air fryer to 300 degrees F or 148 degrees C for a few minutes.
2. Take the crescent dough and unroll it on a flat surface.
3. Cut it into 8 triangles.
4. Sprinkle each triangle with onion powder and generously top them with crumbled bacon bits. Roll up each triangle and gently press the edges to secure.
5. Place the prepared rolls inside the oiled air fryer basket and cook for 12 minutes. Remember to flip them halfway through for even cooking.
6. Once they are beautifully golden and crispy, remove from the air fryer.
7. Serve and savor the deliciousness!

Nutrition Facts:

- Servings: 2
- Calories per serving: 566
- Total Fat: 32.5g (42% Daily Value)
- Total Carbohydrate: 44.7g (16% Daily Value)
- Protein: 21.3g

CHAPTER 3: VEGETABLE RECIPES

Acorn Squash with Cranberries

Preparation Time: 10 Minutes | **Cook Time:** 15 Minutes | **Servings:** 2

Ingredients:

- Salt, to taste
- 4 small acorn squash, steam trimmed, and seeded
- 2 tablespoons of olive oil
- ½ shallot, chopped
- 1 cup of baby Bella mushrooms, chopped
- 1 cup cranberries

Directions:

1. In a mixing bowl, combine all the ingredients listed and toss them thoroughly.
2. Grease the air fryer basket with oil.
3. Place the prepared mixture into the oiled air fryer basket.
4. Cook at 360 degrees F (182 degrees C) for approximately 12-15 minutes.
5. Once done, serve and savor.

Nutrition Facts:

- Servings: 2
- Calories per serving: 281
- Total Fat: 14.1g (18% Daily Value)
- Total Carbohydrate: 37.2g (14% Daily Value)
- Protein: 3.1g

Cheese Zucchini Strips

Preparation Time: 10 Minutes | **Cook Time:** 12 Minutes | **Servings:** 2

Ingredients:

- 1 cup zucchini, sliced into thick strips
- 1 tablespoon olive oil
- 1/4 teaspoon salt
- Black pepper, to taste
- 2 tablespoons parmesan cheese

Directions:

1. Preheat the air fryer to 400 degrees F (204 degrees C) for 3 minutes.
2. In a bowl, combine all the listed ingredients.
3. Transfer the mixed ingredients to the air fryer basket, which has been greased with oil.
4. Cook for 12 minutes at 400 degrees F (204 degrees C).
5. Once finished, serve and savor.

Nutrition Facts:

- Servings: 2
- Calories per serving: 123
- Total Fat: 10.2g (13% Daily Value)
- Total Carbohydrate: 4.3g (2% Daily Value)
- Protein: 5.9g

Parmesan Parsnip Fries

Prep: 10 Minutes | **Cook Time:** 12 Minutes | **Makes:** 4 Servings

Ingredients:

- 1 pound of parsnip, thinly sliced
- 1 teaspoon of garlic powder
- A pinch of sea salt
- 4 tablespoons of hard parmesan cheese
- 2 teaspoons of olive oil

Directions:

1. Begin by preheating your air fryer to 400 degrees F (204 degrees C) for a few minutes.
2. In a mixing bowl, combine all the listed ingredients, ensuring they are well-coated with olive oil and seasonings.
3. Place the parsnip slices into the air fryer basket, lined with parchment paper, and set the temperature to 350 degrees F (176 degrees C).
4. Allow them to cook for 12 minutes, remembering to shake the basket halfway through to ensure even cooking.
5. Once done, carefully remove the air-fried parsnip slices and serve immediately.

Nutrition Facts:

- Servings: 2
- Calories per serving: 305
- Total Fat: 11.4g (15% Daily Value)
- Total Carbohydrate: 42.8g (16% Daily Value)
- Protein: 12g

Vegetable Steak

Preparation Time: 10 Minutes | **Cook Time:** 8-32 Minutes | **Servings:** 4

Ingredients:

- 1 head of cabbage, cut into thick round slices
- 2 tablespoons of butter, or as needed
- 1/4 teaspoon of Old Bay seasoning
- Salt to taste

Directions:

1. Start by adding water under the air fryer basket.
2. Preheat the air fryer to 360 degrees F (182 degrees C) for 5 minutes.
3. Slice the cabbage into thick round slices.
4. Place the cabbage slices in the preheated air fryer basket and top each slice with 1 teaspoon of butter. Sprinkle Old Bay seasoning and a pinch of salt on top.
5. Cook for 8 minutes until the cabbage becomes tender and slightly caramelized.
6. Repeat the process for all the cabbage slices.
7. Serve and enjoy!

Nutrition Facts:

- Servings: 4
- Calories per serving: 96
- Total Fat: 5.9g (8% Daily Value)
- Saturated Fat: 3.7g (19% Daily Value)
- Total Carbohydrate: 10.4g (4% Daily Value)
- Protein: 2.3g

Roasted Air Fryer Sweet Carrots

Preparation Time: 20 Minutes | **Cook Time:** 20 Minutes | **Servings:** 2

Ingredients:

- 1 pound of carrots, washed, peeled, and chopped into 1-inch pieces
- 2 tablespoons of melted butter
- 2 teaspoons of brown sugar
- Salt, to taste

Directions:

1. In a bowl, combine the melted butter, brown sugar, and a pinch of salt.
2. Toss the chopped carrots in the buttery mixture, ensuring they are well-coated.
3. Place the coated carrots into the greased basket of an air fryer.
4. Cook at 400 degrees F (204 degrees C) for 20 minutes, allowing the carrots to roast and caramelize.
5. Once done, transfer to a serving dish and enjoy.

Nutrition Facts:

- Servings: 2
- Calories per serving: 206
- Total Fat: 11.5g (15% Daily Value)
- Total Carbohydrate: 25.3g (9% Daily Value)
- Protein: 2g

Three Cheese Mushrooms

Prep: 8 Minutes | **Cook Time:** 10 Minutes | **Makes:** 1 Serving

Ingredients:

- 6 Portobello mushrooms
- 2 tablespoons olive oil
- 1 cup ricotta cheese
- 6 tablespoons Parmesan cheese (divided)
- 6 tablespoons feta cheese
- 1/4 cup bread crumbs
- 1/4 teaspoon minced fresh rosemary

Directions:

1. Preheat the air fryer for 5 minutes at 375 degrees F (190 degrees C).
2. Remove the upper cap of the mushrooms and lightly coat them with oil spray.
3. In a mixing bowl, combine three types of cheese, bread crumbs, and minced fresh rosemary.
4. Fill the top of each mushroom with the cheese mixture.
5. Place the stuffed mushrooms in the air fryer basket.
6. Cook for 10 minutes at 400 degrees F (204 degrees C).
7. Once cooked, remove from the air fryer, serve, and savor the flavors.

Nutrition Facts:

- Servings: 1
- Calories per serving: 1138
- Total Fat: 73.1g (94% Daily Value)
- Total Carbohydrate: 54.7g (20% Daily Value)
- Protein: 75.8g

Spinach and Cheese Muffins

Prep: 8 Minutes | **Cook Time:** 12 Minutes | **Makes:** 2 Servings

Ingredients:

- 4 strips of breakfast bacon, chopped
- ½ purple onion, chopped
- ½ cups cheddar cheese, shredded
- 1/4 cup of spinach
- 4 large organic eggs
- Salt and black pepper, to taste

Directions:

1. Begin by cooking the chopped breakfast bacon in a skillet until it's crisp. Remove it from the skillet and set it aside.
2. In the same skillet, cook the chopped purple onion until it becomes translucent, then add the spinach. Season the mixture with salt and pepper to taste.
3. In individual ramekins, layer the cooked bacon, followed by the sautéed spinach and onions. Pour one egg into each ramekin and top each with an equal amount of shredded cheddar cheese.
4. Place the ramekins in the air fryer basket and cook for 12 minutes at 375 degrees F (190 degrees C).
5. Once done, remove from the air fryer, serve, and savor your meal.

Nutrition Facts:

- Servings: 2
- Calories per serving: 389
- Total Fat: 28.3g (36% Daily Value)
- Total Carbohydrate: 7.9g (3% Daily Value)
- Protein: 24g

Vegetable Casserole

Preparation Time: 14 Minutes | **Cook Time:** 15 Minutes | **Makes:** 3 Servings

Ingredients:

- 1.5 pounds of green beans, trimmed
- 2 cups of diced mushrooms
- ¼ cup of diced onion
- 2 tablespoons of olive oil
- 2 tablespoons of almond flour
- ¾ cup of vegetable broth
- 1 cup of coconut milk

Directions:

1. Begin by preheating your air fryer to 400 degrees F (204 degrees C) for a few minutes.
2. In a cooking pot, bring water to a boil and add the trimmed green beans. Let them simmer for 6 minutes, then set them aside to drain.
3. In a skillet, sauté the diced onion in olive oil for a few minutes until it becomes translucent. Then, add the vegetable broth and coconut milk. Cook for an additional 5 minutes.
4. Place the blanched green beans and the skillet mixture in an air fryer-safe dish.
5. Cook in the air fryer for 15 minutes at 400 degrees F (204 degrees C).
6. Once it's done cooking, serve and savor the flavors.

Nutrition Facts:

- Servings: 3
- Calories per serving: 384
- Total Fat: 31.5g (40% Daily Value)
- Total Carbohydrate: 24.3g (9% Daily Value)
- Protein: 9.8g

Mushroom and Tofu Stew

Preparation Time: 20 Minutes | **Cook Time:** 35 Minutes | **Servings:** 4

Ingredients:

- 2 tablespoons olive oil
- 1 cup cubed tofu
- Salt, to your taste
- 2 small zucchinis, halved and sliced
- 8 ounces baby Bella mushrooms, quartered
- 12 ounces canned diced tomatoes
- ½ teaspoon red chili powder
- 6 cups of coconut milk

Directions:

1. Begin by preheating the air fryer to 350 degrees F (176 degrees C) for 3 minutes.
2. In a skillet, heat the olive oil and add mushrooms, salt, pepper, zucchini, red chili powder, and diced tomatoes.
3. Cook for 5 minutes, then pour in the coconut milk and bring it to a boil with the lid on top. Afterward, add the tofu.
4. Transfer the mixture to the air fryer basket.
5. Cook it for 20 minutes at 300 degrees F (148 degrees C). Then, serve.

Nutrition Facts:

- Servings: 4
- Calories per serving: 973
- Total Fat: 95.9g (123% Daily Value)
- Total Carbohydrate: 29.3g (11% Daily Value)
- Protein: 16.3g

Blooming Onion

Preparation: 10 Minutes | **Cooking Time:** 12-14 Minutes | **Yields:** 2 Servings

Ingredients:

- 1-2 large white onions
- Salt and black pepper, to taste
- 4 eggs, whisked
- 2 tablespoons olive oil
- 2 cups Panko bread crumbs
- 1 teaspoon garlic powder
- ¼ teaspoon paprika
- 1 cup almond flour
- Oil spray for greasing

Directions:

1. Begin by peeling the onions and cutting the tops off.
2. Slice each onion into 4 sections, leaving about one centimeter at the bottom intact to allow the onion to bloom open.
3. Submerge the sliced onions in ice water for 2 hours to help them open up.
4. In a bowl, mix together salt, garlic powder, paprika, black pepper, and almond flour.
5. Remove the onions from the ice water and pat them dry.
6. Once dry, coat each onion slice in the spicy flour mixture.
7. Crack the eggs into a separate bowl and dip each flour-coated onion slice into the egg mixture.
8. Transfer the Panko bread crumbs and olive oil to another bowl.
9. Coat each onion slice thoroughly with the bread crumbs.
10. Grease a basket with oil spray and place the blooming onions in it.
11. Set the air fryer timer to 22 minutes at 400 degrees F (204 degrees C).
12. Once the onions are crisp and golden, serve them with your favorite dipping sauce.

Nutrition Facts:

- Servings: 2
- Calories per serving: 790
- Total Fat: 35.9g (46% Daily Value)
- Total Carbohydrate: 89.6g (33% Daily Value)
- Protein: 29.6g

CHAPTER 4: POULTRY RECIPES

Chicken   Patties with coleslaw

Preparation Time: 12 Minutes | **Cook Time:** 22 Minutes | **Servings:** 4

Ingredients:

- 1 pound of cooked and shredded chicken
- Salt and black pepper, to taste
- 4 eggs, whisked
- 2 shallots, chopped
- 4 potatoes, boiled and mashed
- 3 green chilies, chopped
- ½ teaspoon coriander powder
- ¼ teaspoon turmeric
- 1 cup Panko breadcrumbs
- Oil spray for greasing

Directions:

1. In a mixing bowl, combine the cooked chicken, chopped shallots, a pinch of salt, black pepper, whisked eggs, mashed potatoes, chopped green chilies, coriander powder, and turmeric. Mix the ingredients thoroughly to form a uniform mixture.
2. Shape the mixture into patties using your hands. Mist the patties with oil spray on both sides.
3. Coat the patties evenly with Panko breadcrumbs.
4. Arrange the coated patties in the air fryer basket, previously greased with cooking spray.
5. Cook the patties in the air fryer at 400 degrees F for 22 minutes, flipping them halfway through the cooking process.
6. Once the patties are golden brown and cooked, remove them from the air fryer, serve, and savor the deliciousness.

Nutrition Facts:

- Calories per serving: 670
- Total Fat: 13.5g (17% Daily Value)
- Saturated Fat: 3.9g (20% Daily Value)
- Cholesterol: 361mg (120% Daily Value)
- Sodium: 424mg (18% Daily Value)
- Total Carbohydrate: 53.4g (19% Daily Value)
- Dietary Fiber: 6.4g (23% Daily Value)
- Total Sugars: 4.7g
- Protein: 79.2g

Sesame Chicken Breast with Cucumber Salad

Preparation Time: 20 Minutes | **Cook Time:** 22 Minutes | **Servings:** 4

Ingredients:

- 1 tablespoon sesame seeds
- 4 tablespoons sesame oil
- 2 tablespoons coconut sugar
- 2 tablespoons coconut amino
- Pinch of salt and black pepper
- 2 tablespoons lemon juice
- 2 pounds chicken breasts

Salad Ingredients:

- ¼ cup sour cream
- 2 tablespoons white wine vinegar
- 2 teaspoons chopped dill weed
- 1 large English cucumber, sliced crosswise into 1/3-inch slices
- 1 large red onion, sliced
- Salt and black pepper, to taste

Directions:

1. In a bowl, whisk together sesame oil, coconut amino, a pinch of salt, black pepper, sesame seeds, coconut sugar, lemon juice, and chicken.
2. Allow the chicken to marinate in this mixture for 30 minutes.
3. Preheat the air fryer to 400 degrees F for a few minutes.
4. Add the marinated chicken to the air fryer basket and cook at 400 degrees F for 22 minutes, flipping it halfway through.
5. In a separate bowl, combine all the salad ingredients.
6. Serve the salad alongside the cooked chicken. Enjoy!

Nutrition Facts:

- Servings: 2
- Calories per serving: 1259
- Total Fat: 71.6g (92% Daily Value)
- Saturated Fat: 17.6g (88% Daily Value)
- Cholesterol: 416mg (139% Daily Value)
- Sodium: 416mg (18% Daily Value)
- Total Carbohydrate: 12.3g (4% Daily Value)
- Dietary Fiber: 3g (11% Daily Value)
- Total Sugars: 4.1g
- Protein: 135.1g

Zesty and Spiced Chicken

Preparation Time: 15 Minutes | **Cook Time:** 25 Minutes | **Makes:** 2 Servings

Ingredients:

- 1.5 pounds boneless and skinless chicken breasts
- 2 cloves of minced garlic
- 1-inch ginger paste
- 1.5 tablespoons lemon juice
- ¼ teaspoon lemon zest
- 2 tablespoons olive oil
- 2 cups plain yogurt
- Salt and black pepper, to taste
- 1 teaspoon red chili powder
- 1 teaspoon turmeric powder
- 1 teaspoon thyme
- 1 teaspoon five-spice powder

Directions:

1. In a bowl, combine minced garlic, ginger paste, lemon juice, lemon zest, olive oil, plain yogurt, salt, black pepper, red chili powder, turmeric powder, thyme, and five-spice powder. Mix well to form a marinade.
2. Coat the chicken breasts thoroughly with the marinade. Marinate the chicken for a minimum of 2 hours in the refrigerator.
3. Preheat your air fryer to 400 degrees F and grease the air fryer basket with oil spray.
4. Place the marinated chicken in the air fryer basket.
5. Cook for 18-25 minutes, flipping the chicken halfway through to ensure even cooking.
6. Once the chicken is cooked and has a golden brown exterior, remove it from the air fryer.
7. Serve the deliciously cooked chicken and enjoy.

Nutrition Facts:

- Servings: 2
- Calories per serving: 957
- Total Fat: 42.7g (55% Daily Value)
- Saturated Fat: 11.5g (58% Daily Value)
- Cholesterol: 317mg (106% Daily Value)
- Sodium: 480mg (21% Daily Value)
- Total Carbohydrate: 20.2g (7% Daily Value)
- Dietary Fibre: 1g (4% Daily Value)
- Total Sugars: 17.6g
- Protein: 112.9g

Sriracha-Honey Wings with blue cheese

Preparation Time: 15 Minutes | **Cook Time:** 20 Minutes | **Servings:** 2

Ingredients:

- 10 chicken wings
- 1/3 cup honey
- 2 tablespoons Sriracha sauce
- 1 tablespoon soy sauce
- 4 tablespoons melted butter
- Salt and black pepper, to taste
- 2 teaspoons lemon juice
- Oil spray, for greasing
- Topping: Blue cheese

Directions:

1. In a large bowl, combine honey, Sriracha sauce, soy sauce, melted butter, salt, pepper, and lemon juice.
2. Heat this mixture over low heat and let it simmer until it reduces by half.
3. While the sauce is simmering, season the chicken wings with salt and pepper and lightly mist them with oil spray.
4. Place the seasoned chicken wings in the air fryer for 15-20 minutes, flipping them halfway through to ensure even cooking.
5. Once the wings are cooked, transfer them to the saucepan and coat them thoroughly with the prepared sauce.
6. Top the coated wings with blue cheese and serve.

Nutrition Facts:

- Servings: 2
- Calories per serving: 900
- Total Fat: 39.95g (51% Daily Value)
- Saturated Fat: 15.6g (78% Daily Value)
- Cholesterol: 358.5mg (120% Daily Value)
- Sodium: 682mg (30% Daily Value)
- Total Carbohydrate: 23.75g (9% Daily Value)
- Dietary Fiber: 0.1g (0% Daily Value)
- Total Sugars: 23.35g
- Protein: 107g

Arugula with Chicken Milanese

Prep: 20 Minutes | **Cook Time:** 12 Minutes | **Makes:** 2 Servings

Ingredients:

- 4 boneless, skinless chicken breasts (16 oz total)
- 1 cup Panko breadcrumbs
- 1 tablespoon poultry seasoning
- 1 tablespoon Italian seasoning
- Salt and black pepper to taste
- 2 tablespoons grated Parmesan cheese
- 2 large eggs, beaten
- 2 teaspoons water
- Olive oil spray
- 6 cups baby arugula
- 4 lemons, cut into wedges

Directions:

1. Preheat the air fryer to 400 degrees F for a few minutes. Meanwhile, cut the chicken breasts into cutlets.
2. Place the chicken cutlets between two sheets of parchment paper and pound them to an even thickness. Season with salt and pepper.
3. In a large bowl, whisk together the beaten eggs and water.
4. In a medium bowl, combine the Panko breadcrumbs, salt, black pepper, Italian seasoning, poultry seasoning, and grated Parmesan cheese.
5. Dip each chicken cutlet into the egg wash, then coat it with the breadcrumb mixture. Make sure to mist both sides of the coated chicken with olive oil spray.
6. Transfer the breaded chicken cutlets to the air fryer basket.
7. Cook for 12 minutes, flipping them halfway through the cooking time.
8. Serve the crispy chicken over a bed of baby arugula and garnish with lemon wedges.
9. If desired, drizzle lemon juice over the chicken.
10. Enjoy your delicious meal!

Nutrition Facts:

- Servings: 2
- Calories per serving: 956
- Total Fat: 39.3g (50% Daily Value)
- Saturated Fat: 13.5g (67% Daily Value)
- Cholesterol: 471mg (157% Daily Value)
- Sodium: 600mg (26% Daily Value)
- Total Carbohydrate: 13.8g (5% Daily Value)
- Dietary Fiber: 1.4g (5% Daily Value)
- Total Sugars: 2.4g
- Protein: 103g

Parmesan Chicken Tenders

Preparation Time: 10 Minutes | **Cook Time:** 12 Minutes | **Makes:** 2 Servings

Ingredients:

- 1 pound skinless chicken breast, cut into strips
- 1 cup grated parmesan cheese
- ½ cup Panko bread crumbs
- 2 eggs
- ½ cup buttermilk
- ¼ teaspoon paprika
- Salt and pepper, to taste
- Oil spray, for greasing

Directions:

1. In a bowl, whisk together eggs and buttermilk.
2. In a separate bowl, combine grated parmesan cheese, salt, pepper, Panko bread crumbs, and paprika.
3. Dip the chicken strips first in the egg wash, and then coat them evenly with the parmesan cheese mixture.
4. Mist the chicken strips with oil spray from all sides.
5. Cook in an air fryer at 400 degrees F for 12 minutes, flipping them halfway through.
6. Once cooked to a golden brown, serve.

Nutrition Facts:

- Servings: 2
- Calories per serving: 898
- Total Fat: 41.5g (53% Daily Value)
- Saturated Fat: 18.7g (93% Daily Value)
- Cholesterol: 428mg (143% Daily Value)
- Sodium: 1299mg (56% Daily Value)
- Total Carbohydrate: 25.9g (9% Daily Value)
- Dietary Fiber: 1.3g (5% Daily Value)
- Total Sugars: 5g
- Protein: 103.8g

Pineapple Marinated Chicken with Rice

Preparation Time: 14 Minutes | **Cook Time:** 22 Minutes | **Servings:** 2

Ingredients:

Marinated Ingredients:

- 1/2 cup of pineapple juice
- 4 tablespoons of ketchup
- 1/3 cup of soy sauce
- 1 tablespoon of dark brown sugar
- Salt, to taste
- 2 tablespoons rice vinegar
- 2 tablespoons fish sauce
- 1 tablespoon olive oil, plus more for cooking
- ½ teaspoon garlic powder
- ½ teaspoon ground cayenne

Other Ingredients:

- 4 large boneless skinless chicken breasts, 6 ounces each
- Oil spray, for greasing
- 2 servings of cooked rice

Directions:

1. In a spacious bowl, whisk together all the marinating ingredients. Allow the chicken to marinate in this mixture for a minimum of 2 hours.
2. Grease the air fryer basket with oil spray and arrange the marinated chicken in it for cooking.
3. Cook in the air fryer for a total of 22 minutes, flipping the chicken halfway through to ensure even cooking.
4. While the chicken is cooking, prepare 2 servings of rice.
5. Once the chicken is cooked to perfection, serve it alongside the cooked rice.

Nutrition Facts:

- Servings: 2
- Calories per serving: 760
- Total Fat: 29.1g (37% Daily Value)
- Saturated Fat: 7g (35% Daily Value)
- Cholesterol: 260mg (87% Daily Value)
- Sodium: 4452mg (194% Daily Value)
- Total Carbohydrate: 28.8g (10% Daily Value)
- Dietary Fiber: 0.6g (2% Daily Value)
- Total Sugars: 23.4g
- Protein: 88.9g

Orange Chicken with cauliflower rice

Preparation: 10 Minutes | **Cook Time:** 22 Minutes | **Servings:** 2

Ingredients:

- 1 pound boneless skinless chicken breasts or chicken thighs
- 2 tablespoons potato starch
- Salt and black pepper, to taste

Orange Sauce:

- 1/2 cup orange juice
- 3 tablespoons brown sugar
- 1 tablespoon soy sauce
- 1 tablespoon lemon juice
- 1 teaspoon orange zest
- 1/4 teaspoon ginger
- 2 teaspoons cornstarch mixed with 2 teaspoons water

2 servings of cauliflower rice, cooked

Directions:

1. Preheat your air fryer to 400 degrees F for 5 minutes.
2. Coat the chicken with potato starch, season with salt and pepper.
3. Place the chicken in the air fryer and cook for 12 minutes, flipping halfway through.
4. In a large bowl, whisk together orange juice, lemon juice, brown sugar, soy sauce, ginger, and orange zest.
5. Simmer the sauce over medium heat in a saucepan. Add the cornstarch-water mixture and cook for an additional 5 minutes until the sauce thickens.
6. Remove the chicken from the air fryer and drizzle it with the prepared orange sauce.
7. Serve the chicken over cooked cauliflower rice.

Nutrition Facts:

- Calories per serving: 518
- Total Fat: 17g (22% Daily Value)
- Saturated Fat: 4.7g (24% Daily Value)
- Cholesterol: 202mg (67% Daily Value)
- Sodium: 652mg (28% Daily Value)
- Total Carbohydrate: 20.9g (8% Daily Value)
- Dietary Fiber: 0.4g (1% Daily Value)
- Total Sugars: 18.6g
- Protein: 66.7g

Hot Buffalo wings with blue cheese dressing

Preparation Time: 15 Minutes | **Cook Time:** 25 Minutes | **Servings:** 4

Ingredients:

- Oil spray, for greasing
- 2 pounds chicken wings, split at the joint
- Salt and black pepper, to taste
- 2 tablespoons of butter
- 1 tablespoon of olive oil
- 1/3 cup hot sauce
- 1 cup blue cheese dressing, for serving
- 2 cups of coleslaw

Directions:

1. In a bowl, combine the butter, salt, pepper, and olive oil. Mix well to create a coating.
2. Coat the chicken wings with the prepared mixture.
3. Arrange the coated wings in an air fryer basket lined with parchment paper.
4. Cook the wings in the air fryer for 25 minutes at 370 degrees F, flipping them halfway through the cooking time.
5. Once cooked to perfection, serve the chicken wings and enjoy them with a side of blue cheese dressing and coleslaw.

Nutrition Facts:

- Servings: 4
- Calories per serving: 1148
- Total Fat: 93g (119% Daily Value)
- Saturated Fat: 23.7g (118% Daily Value)
- Cholesterol: 219mg (73% Daily Value)
- Sodium: 1583mg (69% Daily Value)
- Total Carbohydrate: 13.4g (5% Daily Value)
- Dietary Fiber: 0.1g (0% Daily Value)
- Total Sugars: 1.9g
- Protein: 65g

Hot Parmesan Chicken Wings

Preparation Time: 15 Minutes | **Cook Time:** 25 Minutes | **Makes:** 1 Serving

Ingredients:

- 6 chicken wings
- 1 cup hard Parmesan cheese

Sauce Ingredients:

- 1/4 cup honey
- 1 tablespoon hot sauce
- 1/4 cup soy sauce
- 1 teaspoon sesame oil
- 1/3 teaspoon red pepper flakes
- Salt and black pepper, to taste
- 1/4 teaspoon paprika

Directions:

1. In a bowl, combine all the sauce ingredients.
2. Coat the chicken wings thoroughly with the sauce mixture.
3. Cook the sauced chicken wings in an air fryer at 400 degrees F for 24 minutes, flipping them halfway through the cooking process.
4. Remember to baste the chicken with the prepared sauce after every 8 minutes.
5. Once cooked to perfection, serve and enjoy. Sprinkle some Parmesan cheese on top for added flavor and serve with ranch dressing.

Nutrition Facts:

- Servings: 1
- Calories per serving: 948
- Total Fat: 45.8g (59% Daily Value)
- Saturated Fat: 12.7g (63% Daily Value)
- Cholesterol: 176mg (59% Daily Value)
- Sodium: 4201mg (183% Daily Value)
- Total Carbohydrate: 75.8g (28% Daily Value)
- Dietary Fiber: 1.1g (4% Daily Value)
- Total Sugars: 71g
- Protein: 61.2g

Montréal   Chicken Breasts with chipotle sauce

Prep: 14 Minutes | **Cook Time:** 12 Minutes | **Makes:** 2 Servings

Ingredients:

- 4 large chicken breasts, 6 ounces each
- 2 tablespoons Montreal chicken seasoning
- 1 teaspoon thyme
- 1 teaspoon cumin
- 1/4 teaspoon paprika
- Salt, to taste
- Oil spray, for greasing

Sauce Ingredients:

- 6-ounce chipotles in adobo sauce
- ½ cup sour cream
- 1/3 cup mayonnaise
- 2 tablespoons chopped cilantro
- 1/2 teaspoon cayenne powder
- 1 teaspoon garlic powder
- 1/3 teaspoon cumin
- Salt, to taste

Directions:

1. In a bowl, combine all the sauce ingredients and set it aside for later use.
2. Season the chicken breasts with Montreal chicken seasoning, thyme, cumin, paprika, and salt. Ensure they are well coated.
3. Lightly mist the chicken with oil spray on all sides.
4. Place the seasoned chicken breasts into the air fryer basket.
5. Cook at 390 degrees F for 22 minutes, flipping them halfway through the cooking process.
6. Once cooked, serve the chicken with the prepared sauce.

Nutrition Facts:

- Servings: 4
- Calories per serving: 423
- Total Fat: 23.7g (30% Daily Value)
- Saturated Fat: 7.7g (39% Daily Value)
- Cholesterol: 148mg (49% Daily Value)
- Sodium: 320mg (14% Daily Value)
- Total Carbohydrate: 7g (3% Daily Value)
- Dietary Fiber: 0.3g (1% Daily Value)
- Total Sugars: 1.5g
- Protein: 43.6g

Spicy Chicken Breast with Green Beans

Prep: 20 Minutes | **Cook Time:** 25 Minutes | **Makes:** 2 Servings

Ingredients:

- 4 chicken breasts
- 2 eggs, whisked
- 4 tablespoons of almond milk
- 1 cup of almond flour
- Salt, to taste
- 2 tablespoons of Italian seasoning
- 1 teaspoon of red chili flakes
- Oil spray for greasing
- 1 cup of green beans

Directions:

1. In a bowl, combine the whisked eggs and almond milk.
2. In a separate medium-sized bowl, thoroughly mix almond flour, Italian seasoning, red chili flakes, and salt.
3. Dip each chicken breast into the egg wash, ensuring they are coated, and then coat them in the almond flour mixture.
4. Place the coated chicken breasts into the air fryer basket and cook at 390 degrees F for 25 minutes. Flip the chicken breasts halfway through the cooking time and add the green beans.
5. Continue cooking for the remaining time until the chicken is cooked through and the coating is golden brown.
6. Serve the cooked chicken alongside the green beans.

Nutrition Facts:

- Servings: 2
- Calories per serving: 833
- Total Fat: 44.3g (57% Daily Value)
- Saturated Fat: 14.9g (74% Daily Value)
- Cholesterol: 433mg (144% Daily Value)
- Sodium: 407mg (18% Daily Value)
- Total Carbohydrate: 10.5g (4% Daily Value)
- Dietary Fiber: 4g (14% Daily Value)
- Total Sugars: 3.3g
- Protein: 94.8g

CHAPTER 5: PORK, BEEF, AND LAMB RECIPES

Italian-Style Beef Meatballs

Preparation Time: 26 Minutes | **Cook Time:** 12 Minutes | **Servings:** 2

Ingredients:
- 1 tablespoon of olive oil
- 2 medium shallots, finely minced
- 2 cloves garlic, finely minced
- 1/2 cup Panko breadcrumbs
- 6 tablespoons whole milk
- 1.3 pounds of lean ground beef
- 1 pound of bulk turkey sausage
- 2 large eggs, lightly beaten
- 1/4 cup fresh flat-leaf parsley, finely chopped
- 2 tablespoons rosemary, finely chopped
- 1 tablespoon thyme, finely chopped
- 2 tablespoons Dijon mustard
- Salt, to your taste

Directions:
1. Start by preheating your air fryer to 400 degrees F (204 degrees C).
2. In a skillet, heat the olive oil over medium heat. Add the finely minced shallots and sauté for 2 minutes until they turn translucent. Then, add the finely minced garlic and cook for an additional 2 minutes. Set this mixture aside.
3. In a separate bowl, combine the Panko breadcrumbs and whole milk. Allow them to soak for a few minutes until the breadcrumbs have absorbed the milk.
4. Add the lean ground beef, bulk turkey sausage, lightly beaten eggs, finely chopped fresh parsley, finely chopped rosemary, finely chopped thyme, Dijon mustard, and a pinch of salt to the breadcrumb mixture.
5. Incorporate the cooked shallots and garlic into the mixture.
6. Gently shape the mixture into meatballs, each about 1 1/2 inches in size.
7. Place the meatballs in the air fryer basket and cook at 400°F (204 degrees C) for 12 minutes, or until they are lightly browned and cooked through.
8. Once all the meatballs are cooked, serve and enjoy!

Nutrition Facts:
- Servings: 2
- Calories per serving: 1540
- Total Fat: 103g (132% Daily Value)
- Saturated Fat: 31.5g (158% Daily Value)
- Cholesterol: 640mg (213% Daily Value)
- Sodium: 2147mg (93% Daily Value)
- Total Carbohydrate: 5.7g (2% Daily Value)
- Dietary Fiber: 2.7g (10% Daily Value)
- Total Sugars: 0.6g
- Protein: 141.2g

Beef Stuffed Bell Peppers

Preparation Time: 20 Minutes | **Cook Time:** 20 Minutes | **Servings:** 2

Ingredients:

- 4 large bell peppers
- 1/2 cup cooked rice
- 1 cup cooked minced beef, finely minced
- 1 cup Parmesan cheese
- Salt and black pepper, to taste
- 1 teaspoon cayenne pepper
- ½ teaspoon paprika
- Oil spray for greasing

Directions:

1. Preheat the air fryer to 400 degrees F (204 degrees C) for 2 minutes.
2. Cut the tops off the bell peppers and remove the central core, ensuring all seeds are discarded.
3. In a mixing bowl, combine cooked rice, finely minced cooked beef, Parmesan cheese, salt, black pepper, cayenne pepper, and paprika.
4. Stuff each bell pepper with the mixture, ensuring they are filled to the top.
5. Grease the air fryer basket with oil spray and place the stuffed bell peppers inside.
6. Cook in the air fryer at 400 degrees F (204 degrees C) for 20 minutes.
7. Once done, carefully remove from the air fryer and serve.

Nutrition Facts:

- Servings: 2
- Calories per serving: 1120
- Total Fat: 41g (53% Daily Value)
- Saturated Fat: 21.2g (106% Daily Value)
- Cholesterol: 336mg (112% Daily Value)
- Sodium: 1115mg (48% Daily Value)
- Total Carbohydrate: 59.3g (22% Daily Value)
- Dietary Fiber: 4.3g (15% Daily Value)
- Total Sugars: 12.2g
- Protein: 127.8g

Spicy Beef Fillet

Prep: 10 Minutes | **Cook Time:** 16 Minutes | **Makes:** 1 Serving

Ingredients:

- 1 beef fillet, 8 ounces
- Salt and black pepper, to taste
- 1 tablespoon of melted butter
- 1/2 teaspoon of lemon juice
- 1/2 teaspoon of chopped rosemary
- ½ teaspoon of chopped thyme
- Oil spray for greasing

Directions:

1. Begin by seasoning the 8-ounce beef fillet with a generous pinch of salt, black pepper, lemon juice, chopped thyme, and chopped rosemary. Ensure an even coating of seasoning.
2. Place the seasoned beef fillet into the air fryer and set the temperature to 400 degrees F (204 degrees C). Cook for a total of 16 minutes, making sure to flip the fillet halfway through the cooking time.
3. While cooking, generously top the fillet with the melted butter for added flavor and moisture.
4. Once the beef fillet is done, remove it from the air fryer and let it rest for 5-10 minutes.
5. Serve and savor this delectable dish.

Nutrition Facts:

- Servings: 1
- Calories per serving: 1111
- Total Fat: 52.2g (67% Daily Value)
- Saturated Fat: 23.5g (117% Daily Value)
- Cholesterol: 391mg (130% Daily Value)
- Sodium: 4083mg (178% Daily Value)
- Total Carbohydrate: 16.9g (6% Daily Value)
- Dietary Fiber: 0.5g (2% Daily Value)
- Total Sugars: 16.1g
- Protein: 144.2g

Beef Ribs in Air Fryer

Prep: 10 Minutes | **Cook Time:** 18 Minutes | **Makes:** 2 Servings

Ingredients:

- 4 tablespoons of BBQ sauce
- Salt and black pepper, to taste
- 4 tablespoons brown sugar
- 1.5 pounds of beef ribs, cut into thirds
- Oil spray, for greasing

Directions:

1. Preheat the air fryer to 400 degrees F (204 degrees C) for 2 minutes.
2. In a spacious bowl, season the beef ribs with salt, black pepper, and brown sugar, ensuring they are well coated. Drizzle half of the BBQ sauce over them and mix to evenly distribute.
3. Grease the air fryer basket with oil spray, then add the seasoned beef ribs.
4. Cook at 400 degrees F (204 degrees C) for 16-18 minutes in the air fryer.
5. Once done, serve the beef ribs with the remaining BBQ sauce.

Nutrition Facts:

- **Servings:** 2
- **Amount per serving:**
  - Calories: 750
  - Total Fat: 21.6g (28% Daily Value)
  - Saturated Fat: 8g (40% Daily Value)
  - Cholesterol: 304mg (101% Daily Value)
  - Sodium: 579mg (25% Daily Value)
  - Total Carbohydrate: 29g (11% Daily Value)
  - Dietary Fiber: 0.2g (1% Daily Value)
  - Total Sugars: 25.6g
  - Protein: 103.2g
  - Vitamin D: 0mcg

Sticky Sweet Beef Ribs With Baked Potatoes

Prep: 10 Minutes | **Cook Time:** 16 Minutes | **Makes:** 2 Servings

Ingredients:

- 6 short ribs
- 2 teaspoons minced garlic
- 2 tablespoons olive oil
- 2 tablespoons brown sugar
- 2 tablespoons oyster sauce
- Salt, to taste
- 1 teaspoon sesame oil

Side servings:

- 2 baked potatoes

Directions:

1. Preheat the air fryer to 400 degrees F (204 degrees C) for 5 minutes.
2. In a large bowl, place the short ribs and add all the listed ingredients, including minced garlic, olive oil, brown sugar, oyster sauce, and salt. Toss to coat the ribs evenly.
3. Transfer the seasoned ribs to the air fryer basket and cook them at 400 degrees F (204 degrees C) for 16 minutes.
4. Serve the deliciously cooked short ribs with baked potatoes.

Nutrition Facts:

- **Servings:** 2
- **Calories per serving:** 2481
- **Total Fat:** 144g (185% Daily Value)
- **Saturated Fat:** 48.5g (243% Daily Value)
- **Cholesterol:** 674mg (225% Daily Value)
- **Sodium:** 1379mg (60% Daily Value)
- **Total Carbohydrate:** 73.4g (27% Daily Value)
- **Dietary Fiber:** 6.7g (24% Daily Value)
- **Total Sugars:** 12.3g
- **Protein:** 212g

Prosciutto and Cheese Panini

Preparation Time: 15 Minutes | **Cook Time:** 16 Minutes | **Servings:** 2

Ingredients:

- 4 teaspoons of softened butter
- 4 round slices of Italian sandwich bread
- 2 slices of fresh mozzarella
- 1 roasted red pepper, halved
- 1 cup of prosciutto
- Salt and black pepper, to taste

Directions:

1. Begin by preheating the air fryer to 400 degrees F (204 degrees C) for a few minutes.
2. Take the round sandwich bread slices and generously brush them with the softened butter.
3. Assemble the sandwiches by placing half of the prosciutto, roasted red pepper, and mozzarella slices on two of the bread slices. Season with salt and black pepper.
4. Top each assembled sandwich with the remaining bread slice to create a sandwich.
5. Carefully place the sandwiches in the air fryer basket.
6. Cook at 400 degrees F (204 degrees C) for 14-16 minutes, flipping them halfway through the cooking time.
7. Once cooked to a golden brown perfection, remove them from the air fryer, serve, and savor the flavors.

Nutrition Facts:

- Calories per serving: 249
- Total Fat: 9.8g (13% Daily Value)
- Saturated Fat: 4.6g (23% Daily Value)
- Cholesterol: 36mg (12% Daily Value)
- Sodium: 817mg (36% Daily Value)
- Total Carbohydrate: 24.2g (9% Daily Value)
- Dietary Fiber: 1.2g (4% Daily Value)
- Total Sugars: 1.8g
- Protein: 16.5g

T-Bone Rib in the Air fryer

Preparation Time: 15 Minutes | **Cook Time:** 22 Minutes | **Servings:** 3

Ingredients:

- 1.5 pounds of beef T-bone ribs
- 4 teaspoons of granulated onion
- ½ teaspoon of basil
- 1 teaspoon of red pepper flakes
- 1 tablespoon dry mustard
- Salt and freshly ground black pepper, to taste
- 2 tablespoons of brown sugar
- Oil spray for greasing

Directions:

1. Preheat the air fryer to 400 degrees F (204 degrees C) for 5 minutes.
2. In a mixing bowl, combine all the dry ingredients to create a flavorful rub.
3. Coat the T-bone ribs generously with the rub.
4. Place the seasoned ribs into the air fryer basket, lightly greased with oil spray.
5. Cook for 22 minutes at 400 degrees F (204 degrees C), flipping the ribs halfway through for even cooking.
6. Once done, remove from the air fryer and serve immediately.

Nutrition Facts:

- Servings: 3
- Calories per serving: 646
- Total Fat: 47.5g (61% Daily Value)
- Saturated Fat: 18.2g (91% Daily Value)
- Cholesterol: 171mg (57% Daily Value)
- Sodium: 112mg (5% Daily Value)
- Total Carbohydrate: 7.5g (3% Daily Value)
- Dietary Fiber: 0.7g (3% Daily Value)
- Total Sugars: 6.1g
- Protein: 45.2g

Greek-Style Beef Chops

Preparation: 20 Minutes | **Cook Time:** 12 Minutes | **Servings:** 2

Ingredients:

- 6 tablespoons of Greek yogurt
- 4 tablespoons of fresh cream
- ¼ teaspoon of cumin powder
- 1 tablespoon of crushed coriander seeds
- ½ teaspoon of paprika
- 1 teaspoon of Italian seasoning
- 4 tablespoons of lemon juice
- Salt and black pepper to taste
- 8 beef chops

Directions:

1. In a bowl, combine Greek yogurt and fresh cream. Add cumin powder, crushed coriander seeds, paprika, Italian seasoning, lemon juice, salt, and black pepper. Mix well to create a flavorful marinade.
2. Place the beef chops in the marinade, ensuring they are evenly coated. Refrigerate for a few hours to let the flavors meld.
3. Preheat the air fryer to 400 degrees F (204 degrees C).
4. Arrange the marinated beef chops in the air fryer basket, making sure they are not overcrowded. You may need to cook in batches if necessary.
5. Air fry for 12-16 minutes, flipping the chops halfway through to ensure even cooking and a nice char.
6. Once cooked to your desired doneness, remove from the air fryer.
7. Serve the succulent beef chops immediately.

Nutrition Facts:

- Calories per serving: 504
- Total Fat: 21.2g (27% Daily Value)
- Saturated Fat: 11g (55% Daily Value)
- Cholesterol: 164mg (55% Daily Value)
- Sodium: 2476mg (108% Daily Value)
- Total Carbohydrate: 12.5g (5% Daily Value)
- Dietary Fiber: 0.4g (1% Daily Value)
- Total Sugars: 9.4g
- Protein: 65.2g

Delicious Beef Patties With Rice

Preparation Time: 15 Minutes | **Cook Time:** 22 Minutes | **Makes:** 4 Servings

Ingredients:

- 1 pound minced beef, boneless
- 2 tablespoons avocado oil
- 1/2 cup purple onions, chopped
- 4 green peppers, chopped
- 1 teaspoon Italian seasoning
- 1 teaspoon Old Bay seasoning
- 2 organic eggs, cooked
- 1 tomato, chopped
- Salt and black pepper, to taste
- 2 cups cooked rice

Directions:

1. In a mixing bowl, combine all the listed ingredients thoroughly.
2. Shape the mixture into patties using your hands and allow them to rest for a few minutes.
3. Grease the air fryer basket with oil spray and place the patties inside.
4. Cook for 18-22 minutes at 350 degrees F (198 degrees C), flipping them halfway through.
5. Once cooked to perfection, serve the patties alongside the cooked rice.

Nutrition Facts:

- Servings: 4
- Calories per serving: 836
- Total Fat: 18.4g (24% Daily Value)
- Saturated Fat: 6.5g (33% Daily Value)
- Cholesterol: 285mg (95% Daily Value)
- Sodium: 350mg (15% Daily Value)
- Total Carbohydrate: 82.1g (30% Daily Value)
- Dietary Fiber: 4g (14% Daily Value)
- Total Sugars: 4.3g
- Protein: 79.6g

Teriyaki Style Beef Steak

Preparation Time: 12 Minutes | **Cook Time:** 12 Minutes | **Servings:** 2

Ingredients:

- 1 pound beef Steak

Teriyaki Glaze Ingredients:

- 1/3 cup Soy Sauce
- 1/4 cup Japanese cooking wine
- 1/4 cup Brown Sugar
- 1 tablespoon Lime Juice
- 1/3 cup Orange Juice
- 1 teaspoon ground Ginger
- 1/2 teaspoon Garlic paste

Directions:

1. Preheat the air fryer to 400 degrees F (204 degrees C) for 5 minutes.
2. In a bowl, combine all the teriyaki glaze ingredients and set aside for later use.
3. Place the steak in the air fryer and cook at 400 degrees F (204 degrees C) for 12 minutes, flipping it halfway through.
4. Baste the steak with the teriyaki glaze every 5 minutes during cooking.
5. Once the steak is cooked, let it cool for 10 minutes before serving.

Nutrition Facts:

- Servings: 2
- Calories per serving: 536
- Total Fat: 14.3g (18% Daily Value)
- Saturated Fat: 5.4g (27% Daily Value)
- Cholesterol: 203mg (68% Daily Value)
- Sodium: 2551mg (111% Daily Value)
- Total Carbohydrate: 26.2g (10% Daily Value)
- Dietary Fiber: 0.5g (2% Daily Value)
- Total Sugars: 21.8g
- Protein: 71.9g

Simple And Easy Beef Steak

Prep: 15 Minutes | **Cook Time:** 12 Minutes | **Makes:** 3 Servings

Ingredients:

- 1 cup tamari sauce
- 2-ounce package dry onion soup mix
- 2 pounds beef steak
- 1 teaspoon freshly ground black pepper

Directions:

1. Preheat the air fryer to 400 degrees F (204 degrees C) for 5 minutes.
2. In a bowl, mix the tamari sauce and dry onion soup mix.
3. Coat the beef steak thoroughly with the mixture and let it marinate for 30 minutes.
4. Grease the air fryer basket with oil spray.
5. Place the marinated steak in the air fryer basket.
6. Cook for 12 minutes at 400 degrees F (204 degrees C), flipping the steak halfway through.
7. Once it's cooked to your desired level of doneness, remove it from the air fryer, let it rest for a moment, and then slice and serve. Enjoy!

Nutrition Facts:

- Servings: 2
- Calories per serving: 845
- Total Fat: 28.3g (36% Daily Value)
- Saturated Fat: 10.7g (53% Daily Value)
- Cholesterol: 405mg (135% Daily Value)
- Sodium: 299mg (13% Daily Value)
- Total Carbohydrate: 0.7g (0% Daily Value)
- Dietary Fiber: 0.3g (1% Daily Value)
- Total Sugars: 0g
- Protein: 137.7g

Maple Glazed Rib Eye Steak

Preparation Time: 20 Minutes | **Cook Time:** 10 Minutes | **Servings:** 2

Ingredients:

- Salt and black pepper, to taste
- 1.5 pounds of beef steak
- 1/4 tablespoon minced garlic
- 2 tablespoons of olive oil
- 1 tablespoon lemon juice
- ½ tablespoon chopped fresh rosemary
- ½ cup Maple syrup

Directions:

1. Preheat your air fryer to 400 degrees F (204 degrees C) for 5 minutes.
2. In a mixing bowl, combine the beef steak with a sprinkle of salt, black pepper, minced garlic, lemon juice, fresh rosemary, and olive oil. Make sure the steak is evenly coated.
3. Grease the air fryer basket with oil spray and place the seasoned steak inside the basket.
4. Cook the steak in the air fryer at 400 degrees F (204 degrees C) for 16 minutes, flipping it halfway through to ensure even cooking.
5. Baste the steak with maple syrup every 5 minutes during the cooking process.
6. Once the steak reaches your desired level of doneness, remove it from the air fryer and serve.

Nutrition Facts:

- Servings: 2
- Calories per serving: 964
- Total Fat: 35.6g (46% Daily Value)
- Saturated Fat: 10.2g (51% Daily Value)
- Cholesterol: 304mg (101% Daily Value)
- Sodium: 233mg (10% Daily Value)
- Total Carbohydrate: 53.9g (20% Daily Value)
- Dietary Fiber: 0.4g (1% Daily Value)
- Total Sugars: 47g
- Protein: 103.4g

Garlic Herb Butter Rib Eye

Prep: 12 Minutes | **Cook Time:** 12 Minutes | **Makes:** 2 Servings

Ingredients:

- 3 Rib-eye New York steaks
- 3 tablespoons olive oil
- 2 teaspoons Italian seasoning
- Salt and pepper, to taste

Garlic Herb Butter Ingredients:

- 1/2 cup butter, softened
- 4 garlic cloves, minced
- ½ teaspoon fresh rosemary
- ½ teaspoon fresh thyme
- ½ teaspoon fresh parsley

Directions:

1. In a bowl, mix all the ingredients for the garlic herb butter. Set it aside for later use.
2. Preheat the air fryer to 400 degrees F (204 degrees C) for 5 minutes.
3. Rub each steak with olive oil, Italian seasoning, salt, and pepper.
4. Place the seasoned steaks in the air fryer and cook at 400 degrees F (204 degrees C) for 12 minutes, flipping them halfway through.
5. Once the steaks are cooked to your desired doneness, serve them with a generous dollop of the prepared herbed butter.
6. Allow the butter to melt over the hot steaks and serve.

Nutrition Facts:

- Servings: 2
- Calories per serving: 858
- Total Fat: 73.7g (94% Daily Value)
- Saturated Fat: 32.6g (163% Daily Value)
- Cholesterol: 234mg (78% Daily Value)
- Sodium: 330mg (14% Daily Value)
- Total Carbohydrate: 2g (1% Daily Value)
- Dietary Fiber: 0.3g (1% Daily Value)
- Total Sugars: 0.3g
- Protein: 50.6g

Chipotle New York Steak

Prep: 10 Minutes | **Cook Time:** 14 Minutes | **Makes:** 2 Servings

Ingredients:

- 2 New York steaks, 1 pound
- 1 tablespoon chipotle powder
- 1 tablespoon dark brown sugar
- 1/3 teaspoon cumin
- Oil spray for greasing
- 2 tablespoons olive oil

Directions:

1. Preheat the air fryer to 400 degrees F (204 degrees C) for a few minutes.
2. In a bowl, coat the New York steaks with olive oil, chipotle powder, dark brown sugar, and cumin. Allow them to marinate for a few minutes.
3. Grease the air fryer basket with oil spray and place the seasoned steaks in it.
4. Cook for 14 minutes, flipping the steaks halfway through to ensure even cooking.
5. Once cooked to your desired doneness, remove from the air fryer, serve, and savor the flavors.

Nutrition Facts:

- Servings: 2
- Calories per serving: 591
- Total Fat: 42.4g (54% Daily Value)
- Saturated Fat: 13.1g (65% Daily Value)
- Cholesterol: 150mg (50% Daily Value)
- Sodium: 112mg (5% Daily Value)
- Total Carbohydrate: 4.6g (2% Daily Value)
- Dietary Fiber: 0g (0% Daily Value)
- Total Sugars: 4.4g
- Protein: 50.1g

Steakhouse New York Steak

Preparation Time: 10 Minutes | **Cook Time:** 12-14 Minutes | **Makes:** 2 Servings

Ingredients:

- 4 tablespoons of olive oil
- 2 cloves of garlic
- 1 tablespoon tarragon
- ½ tablespoon rosemary
- Salt and black pepper, to taste
- ½ teaspoon Dijon mustard
- 2 teaspoons of lemon juice
- 1 pound rib-eye steaks
- 1 tablespoon meat rub seasoning

Directions:

1. Preheat your air fryer to 400 degrees F (204 degrees C) for a few minutes.
2. In a bowl, combine the olive oil, minced garlic, tarragon, rosemary, and season with salt and black pepper to taste.
3. Add Dijon mustard and lemon juice to the herb and spice mixture, stirring well.
4. Generously coat the rib-eye steaks with this flavorful rub and let them marinate for 30 minutes.
5. Grease the air fryer basket with oil spray and place the marinated steaks inside.
6. Cook the steaks in the air fryer for 12-14 minutes, flipping them halfway through to ensure even cooking.
7. Once done, remove the steaks from the air fryer and let them rest for a few minutes.
8. Serve and savor the deliciousness.

Nutrition Facts:

- Servings: 2
- Calories per serving: 874
- Total Fat: 78.5g (101% Daily Value)
- Saturated Fat: 24.2g (121% Daily Value)
- Cholesterol: 151mg (50% Daily Value)
- Sodium: 147mg (6% Daily Value)
- Total Carbohydrate: 2.2g (1% Daily Value)
- Dietary Fiber: 0.6g (2% Daily Value)
- Total Sugars: 0.2g
- Protein: 40.7g

CHAPTER 6: SEAFOOD RECIPES

Air Fryer Crab Cakes

Preparation Time: 15 Minutes | **Cook Time:** 10 Minutes | **Makes:** 2 Servings

Ingredients:

- 1 Pound crabmeat
- 1/8 cup Parmesan cheese
- 2 tablespoons mayonnaise
- 1 egg
- 1/4 tablespoon fresh or dried chives
- 1/4 tablespoon fresh or dried dill
- 1 teaspoon Old Bay seasoning
- 1/4 teaspoon salt
- 1/8 teaspoon pepper
- 1/2 cup crushed pork rinds
- Olive oil (to taste)

Directions:

1. Preheat your air fryer at 360 degrees Fahrenheit for 5 minutes.
2. In a mixing bowl, combine the crabmeat, Parmesan cheese, mayonnaise, egg, chives, dill, Old Bay seasoning, salt, and pepper.
3. Form the mixture into equally-sized thick patties.
4. Spray the crab cakes with olive oil and place them in the air fryer basket. Cook for 5 minutes.
5. Flip the crab cakes, lightly spray with olive oil, and continue cooking for another 5 minutes, or until they turn a delightful golden brown.
6. Your delicious crab cakes are now ready to be served.

Nutrition Facts:

- Servings: 2
- Calories per serving: 384
- Total Fat: 13.3g (17% Daily Value)
- Saturated Fat: 3.9g (19% Daily Value)
- Cholesterol: 150mg (50% Daily Value)
- Sodium: 2620mg (114% Daily Value)
- Total Carbohydrate: 37.8g (14% Daily Value)
- Dietary Fiber: 1.2g (4% Daily Value)
- Total Sugars: 15.3g
- Protein: 28g

Delicious Air Fryer Crab Cakes

Preparation Time: 15 Minutes | **Cook Time:** 5-10 Minutes | **Servings:** 2

Ingredients:

- 1 egg
- 2 teaspoons Worcestershire sauce
- 3 tablespoons mayonnaise
- 3-4 teaspoons Dijon mustard

- 2 tablespoons lemon juice
- A dash of sea salt
- 2 teaspoons smoked paprika
- 1 tablespoon Frank's Hot Sauce
- 2 sticks of celery, chopped
- 1 pound of crab meat
- 1/2 cup Panko bread crumbs
- 2-3 tablespoons olive oil or canola oil

Directions:

1. Begin by preheating the air fryer to 390 degrees Fahrenheit.
2. In a mixing bowl, combine the egg, Worcestershire sauce, mayonnaise, Dijon mustard, lemon juice, sea salt, smoked paprika, and chopped celery. Mix thoroughly until well combined.
3. Gently fold in the lump crab meat and Panko breadcrumbs once the mixture is evenly mixed. Use a spoon to create six portions from the mixture.
4. Carefully shape each portion into crab cakes using your hands, being gentle to prevent the lump crab meat from falling apart.
5. Apply a thin layer of oil to the air fryer basket to prevent sticking.
6. Place the crab cakes in the air fryer, ensuring they are not overlapping. Brush a bit of oil over the top of each crab cake.
7. Cook the crab cakes in the air fryer for 5-10 minutes, until they are golden and cooked through.
8. Once done, repeat the process for any remaining crab cakes. Your delicious crab cakes are now ready to be served.

Nutrition Facts:

- Servings: 2
- Calories per serving: 633
- Total Fat: 34.4g (44% Daily Value)
- Saturated Fat: 4.3g (22% Daily Value)
- Cholesterol: 293mg (98% Daily Value)
- Sodium: 2174mg (95% Daily Value)
- Total Carbohydrate: 34.3g (12% Daily Value)
- Dietary Fiber: 2.3g (8% Daily Value)
- Total Sugars: 6g
- Protein: 38.5g

Air-Fryer Wasabi Crabs Cakes

Prep: 15 Minutes | **Cook Time:** 12 Minutes | **Makes:** 2 Servings

Ingredients:

Main:

- 1 finely chopped red pepper
- 1 finely chopped celery rib
- 3 finely chopped green onions
- 2 large egg whites
- 3 tablespoons mayonnaise
- 1/4 teaspoon prepared wasabi
- 1/4 teaspoon salt
- 3/4 cup dry bread crumbs
- 1-1/2 cups drained lump crabmeat
- Cooking spray

For the Sauce:

- 1 chopped celery rib
- 1/3 cup mayonnaise
- 1 chopped green onion
- 1 tablespoon sweet pickle relish
- 1/2 teaspoon prepared wasabi
- 1/4 teaspoon celery salt

Directions:

1. Preheat the air fryer to 300 degrees Fahrenheit.
2. In a mixing bowl, combine all the main ingredients and mix thoroughly.
3. Add 1/3 cup of bread crumbs to the mixture. Stuff the mixture into the crab and shape into patties. Coat the crab cakes with additional bread crumbs.
4. Place the crab cakes in the air fryer basket.
5. Sprinkle the top with cooking spray and cook for 12 minutes.
6. Halfway through cooking, flip the crab cakes and apply cooking spray as needed.
7. For the sauce, place all sauce ingredients in a food processor and pulse until smooth.
8. Serve the crab cakes with the prepared dipping sauce.

Nutrition Facts:

- Servings: 2
- Calories per serving: 439
- Total Fat: 17.2g (22% Daily Value)
- Saturated Fat: 2.7g (13% Daily Value)
- Cholesterol: 95mg (32% Daily Value)
- Sodium: 1218mg (53% Daily Value)
- Total Carbohydrate: 43.6g (16% Daily Value)
- Dietary Fiber: 2.8g (10% Daily Value)
- Total Sugars: 8.2g
- Protein: 27.1g

Air-Fried Crab Sticks

Preparation Time: 15 Minutes | **Cook Time:** 7 Minutes | **Makes:** 2 Servings

Ingredients:
- 250 grams imitation crab sticks
- Cooking spray

Directions:
1. Gently unwrap and unfurl the imitation crab sticks, then cut them into 1 cm wide strips.
2. Place the peeled crab sticks between two large plates. Use cooking spray and tongs to evenly coat them.
3. Preheat the air fryer to 320°F (160°C) for 5 minutes.
4. Put the prepared crab sticks into the air fryer basket.
5. Set the timer for 7 minutes and allow them to cook.
6. To ensure even cooking, gently shake the crab sticks. Once all batches are ready, serve and savor.

Nutrition Facts:
- Servings: 2
- Calories per serving: 113
- Total Fat: 1.4g (2% Daily Value)
- Saturated Fat: 0g (0%)
- Cholesterol: 11mg (4%)
- Sodium: 22mg (1%)
- Total Carbohydrate: 16.5g (6%)
- Dietary Fiber: 0g (0%)
- Total Sugars: 7.8g
- Protein: 7.8g

Air Fryer Frozen Crab Cakes

Preparation Time: 15 Minutes | **Cook Time:** 8 Minutes | **Makes:** 4 Servings

Ingredients:
- 4 Frozen Crab Cakes

Directions:
1. Preheat your air fryer to 375 degrees Fahrenheit for 3-5 minutes.
2. Place the frozen crab cakes into the air fryer basket.
3. Cook the crab cakes for 5-8 minutes.
4. You'll know the crab cakes are ready when they turn a delightful golden brown on the surface.
5. Serve the crab cakes with your preferred sauce, and savor the flavors.

Nutrition Facts:
- Servings: 4
- Calories per serving: 1125
- Total Fat: 50g (64% Daily Value)

- Saturated Fat: 3.2g (16% Daily Value)
- Cholesterol: 0mg (0% Daily Value)
- Sodium: 1938mg (84% Daily Value)
- Total Carbohydrate: 81.3g (30% Daily Value)
- Dietary Fiber: 0g (0% Daily Value)
- Total Sugars: 0g
- Protein: 75g

Crab Cheese Spring Rolls In An Air Fryer

Preparation Time: 15 Minutes | **Cook Time:** 8 Minutes | **Makes:** 2 Servings
Ingredients:
- 12 Spring roll wrappers
- 1 cup Crabmeat
- 8 ounces Cream cheese, softened
- 1 tablespoon Minced Garlic
- 2 tablespoons Olive oil

Directions:
1. In a mixing bowl, combine the crabmeat, softened cream cheese, and minced garlic. Mix thoroughly until well combined.
2. Place hot tap water in a dish and soak one rice paper wrapper for 5-10 seconds until it becomes pliable.
3. Lay the softened wrapper on a plastic board or plate to prevent sticking. Add a portion of the crab and cream cheese mixture onto the wrapper.
4. Roll the wrapper, tucking in the sides, and then roll it up tightly. Repeat this process for the remaining wrappers; this should make approximately 12 spring rolls. Refrigerate them for 30 minutes.
5. After refrigeration, remove the rolls and lightly brush them with olive oil. You can fit six spring rolls in one batch.
6. Arrange the spring rolls in the air fryer basket and cook for 8 minutes at 375 degrees Fahrenheit. Once each batch is done, serve these delightful crab spring rolls and savor the flavor.

Nutrition Facts:
- Servings: 2
- Calories per serving: 1323
- Total Fat: 57.6g (74% Daily Value)
- Saturated Fat: 27.9g (139% Daily Value)
- Cholesterol: 193mg (64% Daily Value)
- Sodium: 3579mg (156% Daily Value)
- Total Carbohydrate: 153.8g (56% Daily Value)

- Dietary Fiber: 4.8g (17% Daily Value)
- Total Sugars: 16.2g
- Protein: 47.1g

Frozen Crab Cakes In Air Fryer

Preparation Time: 15 Minutes | **Cook Time:** 8 Minutes | **Servings:** 2

Ingredients:
- 4 Phillips Frozen Crab Cakes

Directions:
1. Begin by preheating the air fryer to 375 degrees Fahrenheit for 5 minutes.
2. Place the frozen crab cakes in the air fryer basket.
3. After 5 minutes, check the crab cakes to ensure even cooking.
4. Continue to cook the crab cakes for an additional 5 to 8 minutes or until they are golden and crispy.
5. Once fully cooked, remove them from the air fryer and serve to savor the deliciousness.

Nutrition Facts:
- Servings: 2
- Calories per serving: 186
- Total Fat: 9g (12% Daily Value)
- Saturated Fat: 1.8g (9% Daily Value)
- Cholesterol: 180mg (60% Daily Value)
- Sodium: 396mg (17% Daily Value)
- Total Carbohydrate: 0.6g (0% Daily Value)
- Dietary Fiber: 0g (0% Daily Value)
- Total Sugars: 0g
- Protein: 24.3g

Air Fryer Crab Cake Fritters

Preparation Time: 12 Minutes | **Cook Time:** 14 Minutes | **Makes:** 2 Servings

Ingredients:

- 1 (12 ounces) can of lump crab meat
- 3 tablespoons of breadcrumbs
- Salt to taste
- Pepper to taste
- 2 whisked eggs

Directions:

1. Start by gently coating the interior of the air fryer with a nonstick spray.
2. In a mixing bowl, combine all the ingredients thoroughly. Use your hands to form golf ball-sized balls from the mixture.

3. Place the crab cake balls into the air fryer and cook at 350 degrees for 14 minutes, or until they turn beautifully golden and crispy.
4. Your delicious crab cakes are now ready to be served.

Nutrition Facts:

- Servings: 2
- Calories per serving: 363
- Total Fat: 29.5g (38% Daily Value)
- Saturated Fat: 5.9g (30% Daily Value)
- Cholesterol: 496mg (165% Daily Value)
- Sodium: 1323mg (58% Daily Value)
- Total Carbohydrate: 12g (4% Daily Value)
- Dietary Fiber: 0.5g (2% Daily Value)
- Total Sugars: 2.2g
- Protein: 39.1g

Air Fryer Low Country Boil

Preparation Time: 10 Minutes | **Cook Time:** 15 Minutes | **Servings:** 2
Ingredients:
- 1 cup water
- 8 clams
- 2 pounds sausage
- 3 lobster tails
- 2 half-cut lemons
- 3 half-cut ears of corn
- 1 pound shrimp
- 2 tablespoons of boil seasoning

Directions:
1. Preheat the air fryer at 400 degrees Fahrenheit for 4 minutes.
2. Place 1 cup of water into the basket of the air fryer, and set the temperature to 400 degrees Fahrenheit. Add all the listed ingredients.
3. Cook the ingredients for 15 minutes at 400 degrees Fahrenheit.
4. Serve hot and savor the flavors.

Nutrition Facts:
- Servings: 2
- Calories per serving: 2549
- Total Fat: 139g (178% Daily Value)
- Saturated Fat: 44.2g (221% Daily Value)
- Cholesterol: 1975mg (658% Daily Value)
- Sodium: 8112mg (353% Daily Value)
- Total Carbohydrate: 16.7g (6% Daily Value)
- Dietary Fiber: 0.5g (2% Daily Value)
- Total Sugars: 4g
- Protein: 285.9g

Panko-Breaded Fried Razor Clams

Preparation Time: 15 Minutes | **Cook Time:** 8 Minutes | **Makes:** 2 Servings
Ingredients:
- 6 razor clams
- 2 eggs
- 1 cup all-purpose flour
- Salt, to taste
- Freshly ground black pepper, to taste
- Garlic powder, to taste
- 1 cup Panko breadcrumbs
- ¼ cup shredded Parmesan cheese

Directions:
1. Start by cleaning the razor clams.
2. Place wax paper on a flat baking sheet. Then, whisk the eggs in a large bowl.

3. In a separate bowl, combine the all-purpose flour, salt, freshly ground black pepper, and garlic powder.
4. In another bowl, mix the Panko breadcrumbs and shredded Parmesan cheese.
5. Dip the cleaned clams into the beaten eggs, ensuring they are well-coated, and then roll them in the Panko breadcrumb and Parmesan mixture. Place them on the prepared baking sheet.
6. Freeze the baking sheet until the clams become firm.
7. Preheat the air fryer to 400 degrees Fahrenheit (200 degrees Celsius).
8. Cook the clams in the air fryer for 8 minutes until they are crispy and golden brown.
9. Your delectable clams are now ready to be served.

Nutrition Facts:
- Servings: 2
- Calories per serving: 672
- Total Fat: 17.3g (22% Daily Value)
- Saturated Fat: 8.2g (41% Daily Value)
- Cholesterol: 208mg (69% Daily Value)
- Sodium: 950mg (41% Daily Value)
- Total Carbohydrate: 89.7g (33% Daily Value)
- Dietary Fiber: 4.1g (15% Daily Value)
- Total Sugars: 3.9g
- Protein: 38.3g

Sweet & Spicy Mussels

Preparation: 15 Minutes | **Cook Time:** 7 Minutes | **Servings:** 4
Ingredients:
- 1 pound Blue Mussels
- 2 teaspoons Granulated Sugar
- 1/4 cup Mayonnaise
- 2 tablespoons chopped Fresh Scallion
- Juice of 1 Persian Lime
- 2 tablespoons Sweet Chili Sauce

Directions:
1. Begin by washing the mussels thoroughly in cold water.
2. In a medium mixing bowl, combine all the ingredients. Then, drizzle half of the sauce mixture over the mussels and gently toss to coat them.
3. Place the mussels into the air fryer basket.
4. Cook the mussels for 5 to 7 minutes at 390°Fahrenheit, or until they have opened.
5. Once cooked, carefully remove the mussels from their shells.
6. Serve the mussels with the remaining sauce and savor the flavors.

Nutrition Facts:
- Servings: 4
- Calories per serving: 471
- Total Fat: 15.1g (19% Daily Value)
- Saturated Fat: 2.7g (13% Daily Value)
- Cholesterol: 131mg (44% Daily Value)

- Sodium: 1002mg (44% Daily Value)
- Total Carbohydrate: 25.5g (9% Daily Value)
- Dietary Fiber: 0.1g (0% Daily Value)
- Total Sugars: 6g
- Protein: 54.2g

Clams In The Air Fryer

Preparation Time: 15 Minutes | **Cook Time:** 5 Minutes | **Makes:** 4 Servings
Ingredients:
- 1 cup bread crumbs
- Salt and black pepper, to taste
- ½ cup mozzarella cheese
- 1.2 cup fresh parsley
- ½ teaspoon lemon zest
- 6 tablespoons of melted butter
- 2 garlic cloves
- 1 dozen clams
- 1 lemon, wedges

Directions:
1. In a mixing bowl, combine mozzarella cheese, bread crumbs, lemon zest, minced garlic, fresh parsley, and melted butter. Thoroughly mix the ingredients until well combined.
2. Open the clams and place them in a large bowl.
3. Stuff each clam with the breadcrumb mixture prepared in step 1.
4. Season the stuffed clams with salt and black pepper according to your taste.
5. Preheat your air fryer to 400 degrees Fahrenheit (200 degrees Celsius).
6. Place the stuffed clams in the air fryer basket and cook for 5 minutes until they are crispy and golden.
7. Once cooked, serve the stuffed clams with lemon wedges.

Nutrition Facts:
- Servings: 4
- Calories per serving: 323
- Total Fat: 20.1g (26% Daily Value)
- Saturated Fat: 11.7g (59% Daily Value)
- Cholesterol: 68mg (23% Daily Value)
- Sodium: 386mg (17% Daily Value)
- Total Carbohydrate: 22.8g (8% Daily Value)
- Dietary Fiber: 1.9g (7% Daily Value)
- Total Sugars: 1.9g
- Protein: 13.1g

Ginger Garlic Shrimp

Preparation Time: 15 Minutes | **Cook Time:** 10 Minutes | **Makes:** 2 Servings

Ingredients:
- 12 large shrimp
- 2 tablespoons of oyster sauce
- 2 finely chopped garlic cloves
- 2-inch finely chopped ginger
- 2 tablespoons of butter
- Salt, to taste
- Pepper, to taste

Directions:
1. In a large bowl, combine all the ingredients and mix thoroughly.
2. Place the shrimp mixture in the air fryer basket.
3. Cook for 10 minutes at 400 degrees Fahrenheit.
4. Serve hot and savor the flavors.

Nutrition Facts:
- **Servings:** 2
- Calories per serving: 148
- Total Fat: 12.1g (16% Daily Value)
  - Saturated Fat: 7.5g (37% Daily Value)
  - Cholesterol: 100mg (33% Daily Value)
  - Sodium: 350mg (15% Daily Value)
- Total Carbohydrate: 2g (1% Daily Value)
  - Dietary Fiber: 0.1g (0% Daily Value)
  - Total Sugars: 0g
- Protein: 7.9g

CHAPTER 7: SNACKS, SANDWICHES AND WRAPS

Vegetable Biscuits

Preparation Time: 15 Minutes | **Cook Time:** 16 Minutes | **Servings:** 2

Ingredients:

½ cup broccoli

½ cup cauliflower

3 chopped garlic cloves

2 large eggs

½ cup shredded cheddar cheese

½ cup low-fat plain Greek yogurt

1/3 cup diced scallions

Cooking spray

Required salt and black pepper

Oil spray

Directions:

Begin by preheating your air fryer to 400 degrees F or 204 degrees C for 3 minutes.

Steam the cauliflower and broccoli florets until tender, then set them aside.

In a mixing bowl, combine the steamed cauliflower and broccoli with the chopped garlic cloves, large eggs, shredded cheddar cheese, low-fat plain Greek yogurt, diced scallions, and season with salt and black pepper to taste. Mix everything thoroughly.

Grease four ramekins with oil spray.

Transfer the prepared batter into the greased ramekins.

Place the ramekins in the air fryer and cook for 16 minutes at 350 degrees F or 176 degrees C, or until the biscuits are cooked through and have a golden-brown crust.

Once done, remove the savory biscuits from the air fryer, serve, and enjoy.

Nutrition Facts:

Servings: 2

Amount per serving:

Calories: 241

Total Fat: 15.1g (19% Daily Value)

Saturated Fat: 7.6g (38% Daily Value)

Cholesterol: 218mg (73% Daily Value)

Sodium: 286mg (12% Daily Value)

Total Carbohydrate: 8.8g (3% Daily Value)

Dietary Fiber: 1.7g (6% Daily Value)

Total Sugars: 4.2g

Protein: 18.6g

BBQ And Paprika Chickpeas With Tofu
Preparation Time: 15 Minutes | **Cook Time:** 16 Minutes | **Servings:** 2

Ingredients:

1 teaspoon paprika

½ teaspoon brown sugar

½ teaspoon celery salt

½ teaspoon dry mustard

1 cup tofu

2 cups of chickpeas

Oil spray

Directions:

Begin by preheating your air fryer to 400 degrees F or 204 degrees C for 2 minutes.

In a bowl, combine the paprika, brown sugar, celery salt, and dry mustard, creating a flavorful spice mix.

Toss the chickpeas and tofu in the spice mix, ensuring they are evenly coated.

Grease the air fryer basket with oil spray and add the seasoned chickpeas and tofu.

Cook for 16 minutes at 390 degrees F or 198 degrees C, or until they turn crispy and golden brown.

Once done, remove them from the air fryer and serve. Enjoy your delicious, crispy chickpeas and tofu!

Nutrition Facts:

Servings: 2

Amount per serving:

Calories: 829

Total Fat: 18g (23% Daily Value)

Saturated Fat: 2.4g (12% Daily Value)

Cholesterol: 0mg (0% Daily Value)

Sodium: 66mg (3% Daily Value)

Total Carbohydrate: 125.1g (45% Daily Value)

Dietary Fiber: 36.5g (130% Daily Value)

Total Sugars: 23.1g

Protein: 49.3g

Cheese-Filled Eggplants

Preparation Time: 15 Minutes | **Cook Time:** 25 Minutes | **Servings:** 2

Ingredients:

1 eggplant

2 tbsp Olive Oil

Sea salt (to taste)

1 cup tomatoes

1/2 cup chopped mint leaves

1 tsp ginger garlic paste

1 finely chopped onion

1 cup cooked shredded chicken

1/4 cup Parmesan cheese

Directions:

Begin by preheating your air fryer to 400 degrees F or 204 degrees C.

Cut the eggplant in half lengthwise and scoop out the flesh from the center, leaving a shell.

In a skillet, heat the olive oil and sauté the finely chopped onion until it becomes translucent.

Add the ginger garlic paste, tomatoes, and chopped mint leaves to the skillet. Season with sea salt and cook for 5-7 minutes until the tomatoes break down and the mixture becomes fragrant.

Stir in the cooked shredded chicken and continue to cook for an additional 5-7 minutes. Turn off the heat and allow the mixture to cool slightly.

Once the mixture has cooled, stuff the hollowed eggplant halves with this filling.

Sprinkle Parmesan cheese on top of the stuffed eggplants.

Place the stuffed eggplants in the air fryer basket and cook for 14-16 minutes at 400 degrees F or 204 degrees C until the eggplants become tender and the cheese is golden and bubbly.

Once cooked, carefully remove the stuffed eggplants from the air fryer, serve, and enjoy your delicious meal.

Nutrition Facts:

Servings: 2

Amount per serving:

Calories: 411

Total Fat: 17.5g (22% Daily Value)

Saturated Fat: 2.7g (13% Daily Value)

Cholesterol: 54mg (18% Daily Value)

Sodium: 69mg (3% Daily Value)

Total Carbohydrate: 42.8g (16% Daily Value)

Dietary Fiber: 23.2g (83% Daily Value)

Total Sugars: 21.1g

Protein: 27.8g

Oats Biscuits

Preparation Time: 15 Minutes | **Cook Time:** 15 Minutes | **Servings:** 2

Ingredients:

1.5 cups plain flour

1/4 cup butter

1/4 cup white sugar

2 small eggs

1/4 cup desiccated coconut

1 cup oats

1 cup white chocolate

1/2 teaspoon vanilla extract

Directions:

In a large bowl, use a hand beater to whisk together the butter and sugar until well combined.

Add the small eggs to the mixture and continue to whisk until the mixture is smooth and creamy.

Now, incorporate the desiccated coconut, oats, white chocolate chunks, and vanilla extract into the mixture. Stir until all the ingredients are evenly distributed.

Gradually add the plain flour and mix until a dough forms.

Shape the dough into biscuit (cookie) shapes. You can use your hands or a cookie cutter to create desired shapes.

Preheat your Air Fryer to 375 degrees F (190 degrees C).

Place the shaped biscuits onto the air fryer tray or basket in a single layer, ensuring they are not overcrowded.

Bake the biscuits in the Air Fryer for 15 minutes, or until they turn golden brown.

Once done, remove the hot biscuits from the Air Fryer and let them cool slightly.

Serve your freshly baked coconut oat biscuits and savor the deliciousness.

Nutrition Facts:

Servings: 2

Amount per serving:

Calories: 1494

Total Fat: 75.8g (97% Daily Value)

Saturated Fat: 49g (245% Daily Value)

Cholesterol: 217mg (72% Daily Value)

Sodium: 307mg (13% Daily Value)

Total Carbohydrate: 181.7g (66% Daily Value)

Dietary Fiber: 11.4g (41% Daily Value)

Total Sugars: 78.3g

Protein: 26.9g

Creamy Tomato Soup

Preparation Time: 15 Minutes | **Cook Time:** 9 Minutes | **Servings:** 1

Ingredients:

1 cup of tomato soup

1/4 cup of coconut milk

1/2 cup sour cream

2 basil leaves

Salt and black pepper

Directions:

Select a round pan that fits comfortably inside your air fryer.

In the pan, combine the tomato soup, coconut milk, salt, and black pepper.

Place the pan with the soup mixture into the air fryer.

Cook the soup at 375 degrees F or 190 degrees C for 9 minutes in the air fryer.

Once the soup is fully cooked, serve it piping hot, garnished with basil leaves and a generous dollop of sour cream.

Nutrition Facts:

Servings: 1

Amount per serving:

Calories: 397

Total Fat: 25.5g (33% Daily Value)

Saturated Fat: 15.4g (77% Daily Value)

Cholesterol: 51mg (17% Daily Value)

Sodium: 1444mg (63% Daily Value)

Total Carbohydrate: 38.7g (14% Daily Value)

Dietary Fiber: 3.1g (11% Daily Value)

Total Sugars: 20.5g

Protein: 7.7g

Every Thing Bagel Brussels sprouts

Preparation Time: 15 Minutes | **Cook Time:** 15 Minutes | **Servings:** 2

Ingredients:

26 ounces of Brussels sprouts

2 tablespoons of avocado oil

½ teaspoon of regular sesame seeds

½ teaspoon of garlic powder

½ teaspoon of onion powder

¼ cup of Parmesan cheese

¼ cup of almonds

Salt (to taste)

½ teaspoon of black sesame seeds

2 tablespoons of bagel seasoning

Directions:

Begin by adding water to a cooking pot and cooking the Brussels sprouts for 10 minutes. Once done, set them aside and cut the Brussels sprouts in half.

In a bowl, combine the avocado oil, almonds, salt, Parmesan cheese, and all the listed ingredients. Mix everything thoroughly.

Place the mixture into the air fryer basket.

Cook the Brussels sprout mixture in the air fryer for 15 minutes at 400 degrees F or 204 degrees C.

Once the cooking is complete, serve your delicious Brussels sprouts with Parmesan and almond topping, and savor the flavors.

Nutrition Facts:

Servings: 2

Amount per serving:

Calories: 345

Total Fat: 15.4g (20% Daily Value)

Saturated Fat: 5.3g (26% Daily Value)

Cholesterol: 20mg (7% Daily Value)

Sodium: 431mg (19% Daily Value)

Total Carbohydrate: 39g (14% Daily Value)

Dietary Fiber: 16.1g (58% Daily Value)

Total Sugars: 8.9g

Protein: 24.6g

Cauliflower Au Gratin
Preparation Time: 15 Minutes | **Cook Time:** 28 Minutes | **Servings:** 2

Ingredients:

2 tablespoons butter

1 small onion, chopped

2 teaspoons xanthan gum

1 cup cream

1 cup sour cream

½ pounds of bacon

2 cups shredded cheddar cheese

½ cup shredded Parmesan cheese

2 cups chopped cauliflower

Salt and black pepper to taste

1 tablespoon garlic powder

1 chopped scallion

Directions:

Begin by preheating your air fryer to 400 degrees F or 204 degrees C.

Boil the chopped cauliflower in water for 8-10 minutes until it's tender. Drain and set aside.

In a skillet, melt the butter and sauté the chopped onions until they become translucent.

Sprinkle xanthan gum over the onions and stir to combine.

Add the cream and sour cream to the skillet, then turn off the heat. Transfer this mixture to a separate bowl.

Add the cooked cauliflower to the bowl with the cream mixture. Set it aside.

Using a spoon or your hands, thoroughly mash the cauliflower in the bowl. Add garlic powder, salt, and black pepper, and mix well.

Transfer this cauliflower mixture into a casserole dish.

Top the cauliflower mixture with shredded cheddar cheese, crumbled bacon, shredded Parmesan cheese, and chopped scallion.

Place the casserole dish in the air fryer and cook for 12-15 minutes, until the cheese is melted and bubbly, and the casserole is heated through.

Serve the delicious cauliflower casserole hot.

Nutrition Facts:

Servings: 2

Amount per serving:

Calories: 1424

Total Fat: 106.8g (137% Daily Value)

Saturated Fat: 53g (265% Daily Value)

Cholesterol: 282mg (94% Daily Value)

Sodium: 3917mg (170% Daily Value)

Total Carbohydrate: 26.2g (10% Daily Value)

Dietary Fiber: 3.9g (14% Daily Value)

Total Sugars: 8.3g

Protein: 91g

Coconut Pudding With Buns

Preparation Time: 15 Minutes | **Cook Time:** 16 Minutes | **Servings:** 2

Ingredients:

1/3 cup organic applesauce

3/4 cup coconut cream

3/4 cup shredded coconut flakes

2 tablespoons brown sugar

Pinch of salt

4 whole-grain buns

Oil spray

Directions:

In a mixing bowl, combine the organic applesauce, coconut cream, shredded coconut flakes, brown sugar, and a pinch of salt. Whisk the mixture thoroughly until well combined.

Pour the prepared mixture into a round pan. Tear the whole-grain buns into pieces and add them to the mixture in the pan.

Place the pan in an air fryer and cook for 16 minutes at 400 degrees F or 204 degrees C.

Once the coconut and apple bread pudding is cooked to a delightful golden-brown perfection, remove it from the air fryer.

Serve your delicious creation and savor the flavors.

Nutrition Facts:

Servings: 2

Amount per serving:

Calories: 432

Total Fat: 32.6g (42% Daily Value)

Saturated Fat: 28g (140% Daily Value)

Cholesterol: 0mg (0% Daily Value)

Sodium: 235mg (10% Daily Value)

Total Carbohydrate: 34g (12% Daily Value)

Dietary Fiber: 7.1g (25% Daily Value)

Total Sugars: 17.1g

Protein: 7.1g

Zucchini Noodles With Basil And Cherry Tomatoes

Preparation Time: 15 Minutes | **Cook Time:** 20 Minutes | **Servings:** 2

Ingredients:

2 teaspoons of avocado oil

2 large zucchinis

Salt and black pepper, to taste

1 cup vegan cheese

1 cup cherry tomatoes

2 tablespoons of balsamic vinegar

1 tablespoon of basil leaves

Directions:

Start by spiralizing the zucchinis using a colander.

Sprinkle the spiralized zucchinis with salt and allow them to sit for 30 minutes to release excess moisture.

After the 30 minutes, squeeze and drain the zucchinis thoroughly. Then, place them in the air fryer basket along with the cherry tomatoes. Season the mixture with black pepper to taste.

Toss the zucchinis and cherry tomatoes together and cook them in the air fryer for 20 minutes at 375 degrees F or 190 degrees C.

Once cooked, serve the zucchini and cherry tomatoes hot, drizzled with balsamic vinegar, sprinkled with vegan cheese, and garnished with fresh basil leaves.

Enjoy this flavorful dish immediately.

Nutrition Facts:

Servings: 2

Amount per serving:

Calories: 528

Total Fat: 41.4g (53% Daily Value)

Saturated Fat: 15.3g (76% Daily Value)

Cholesterol: 0mg (0% Daily Value)

Sodium: 613mg (27% Daily Value)

Total Carbohydrate: 29.8g (11% Daily Value)

Dietary Fiber: 14.9g (53% Daily Value)

Total Sugars: 13g

Protein: 14.8g

CHAPTER 8: PIZZAS & BREADS

Keto Air Fryer Roll Bread

Preparation Time: 12 Minutes | **Cook Time:** 10 Minutes | **Servings:** 4

Ingredients:

1 cup almond flour

2 cups shredded mozzarella cheese

4 tablespoons butter

1 and 1/2 teaspoons baking powder

1 teaspoon vinegar

1 egg

1 tablespoon butter

Directions:

In a microwave-safe bowl, combine almond flour, shredded mozzarella cheese, and 2 tablespoons of butter. Microwave the mixture until the cheese and butter are fully melted.

Create the dough by adding baking powder and vinegar to the melted mixture. Mix well until a dough forms.

Once the dough is ready, divide it into equal-sized balls. Allow the dough to rest for 5 minutes.

Prepare an egg wash by adding the melted butter to the egg and mixing it together.

Apply the egg wash mixture onto the dough rolls.

Line the air fryer basket with parchment paper and arrange the rolls in the air fryer.

Set the air fryer to cook for 10 minutes at 350 degrees F (170 degrees C).

When the rolls are halfway cooked, flip them and continue baking until they are golden brown and fully cooked.

Serve the hot almond flour rolls and savor their deliciousness.

Nutrition Facts:

Servings: 4

Amount per serving:

Calories: 244

Total Fat: 22.5g (29% Daily Value)

Saturated Fat: 9.8g (49% Daily Value)

Cholesterol: 80mg (27% Daily Value)

Sodium: 192mg (8% Daily Value)

Total Carbohydrate: 4.3g (2% Daily Value)

Dietary Fiber: 1.5g (5% Daily Value)

Total Sugars: 0.6g

Protein: 8.6g

Air Fryer Keto Garlic Cheese 'Bread'

Preparation Time: 15 Minutes | **Cook Time:** 10 Minutes | **Servings:** 2

Ingredients:

1-1/4 cup mozzarella cheese

1/4 cup grated Parmesan cheese

1 organic egg

1/2 teaspoon garlic powder

Directions:

Begin by placing parchment paper in the air fryer basket.

In a mixing bowl, combine the mozzarella cheese, grated Parmesan cheese, organic egg, and garlic powder. Thoroughly mix these ingredients until well combined.

Shape the dough into a circle on the parchment paper inside the air fryer basket.

Preheat the air fryer to 350 degrees Fahrenheit or 170 degrees Celsius.

Bake the garlic cheese bread in the air fryer for 10 minutes or until it turns golden brown and becomes fragrant.

Once done, remove the garlic cheese bread from the air fryer, and serve it warm to enjoy.

Nutrition Facts:

Servings: 2

Amount per serving:

Calories: 164

Total Fat: 10.7g (14% Daily Value)

Saturated Fat: 6.2g (31% Daily Value)

Cholesterol: 109mg (36% Daily Value)

Sodium: 376mg (16% Daily Value)

Total Carbohydrate: 2.2g (1% Daily Value)

Dietary Fiber: 0.1g (0% Daily Value)

Total Sugars: 0.3g

Protein: 15.9g

Air Fryer Apple Streusel Quick Bread

Preparation Time: 10 Minutes | **Cook Time:** 20 Minutes | **Servings:** 4

Ingredients:

Streusel Topping:

>
> 1/2 cup brown sugar
>
> 1 teaspoon ground cinnamon
>
> 1 teaspoon ground nutmeg

Apple Quick Bread:

>
> 2 apples, peeled and diced
>
> 2/3 cup sugar
>
> 1/2 cup butter
>
> 2 eggs
>
> 1 teaspoon vanilla extract
>
> 1 1/2 cups all-purpose flour
>
> 1 teaspoon baking powder
>
> 1 teaspoon baking soda
>
> 1/2 cup sour cream

Directions:

Grease the baking pan with olive oil.

In a mixing bowl, combine the brown sugar, cinnamon, and nutmeg. Mix thoroughly. Peel and chop the apples, toss them with 1 tablespoon of sugar, and add them to the mixing bowl. Mix well.

In another bowl, combine sour cream, sugar, butter, eggs, and vanilla extract. Mix until well combined. Gradually add in the flour, baking powder, and baking soda.

Pour half of the batter into the prepared baking pan. Sprinkle the apple mixture evenly, then pour the remaining batter on top.

Top the bread with the brown sugar, cinnamon, and nutmeg mixture.

Place the pan in the air fryer basket and cook for 12-20 minutes at 350 degrees F or 170 degrees C, or until the bread is thoroughly cooked.

Once done, remove from the air fryer, serve, and enjoy!

Nutrition Facts:

Servings: 4

Amount per serving:

        Calories: 728

        Total Fat: 32.1g (41% Daily Value)

        Saturated Fat: 19.2g (96% Daily Value)

        Cholesterol: 156mg (52% Daily Value)

        Sodium: 533mg (23% Daily Value)

        Total Carbohydrate: 105.2g (38% Daily Value)

        Dietary Fiber: 4.4g (16% Daily Value)

        Total Sugars: 63.2g

        Protein: 9.1g

Cheesy Sweet And Savory Garlic Bread

Preparation Time: 12 Minutes | **Cook Time:** 5 Minutes | **Servings:** 2

Ingredients:

1 whole baguette

5 tablespoons chopped coriander leaves

5 tablespoons condensed milk

5 tablespoons vegan butter

1 teaspoon oregano

1 teaspoon red chili flakes

5 cloves garlic, minced

1 cup grated cheese or vegan cheese

Directions:

Begin by cutting the baguette into slices.

In a mixing bowl, combine melted unsalted butter, minced garlic cloves, chopped coriander leaves, oregano, and red chili flakes.

Pour the condensed milk into the mixture and whisk until well combined.

Brush the baguette slices generously with the prepared mixture.

Sprinkle the grated cheese or vegan cheese on top of the baguette slices as toppings.

Preheat your air fryer and lightly spray it with oil.

Place the dressed baguette slices in the air fryer.

Set the air fryer timer to 5 minutes at 350°F (170°C) or until the baguette slices turn golden and crispy.

Once done, serve the garlic and cheese baguette slices hot and enjoy!

Nutrition Facts:

Servings: 2

Amount per serving:

Calories: 524

Total Fat: 45.5g (58% Daily Value)

Saturated Fat: 22.5g (112% Daily Value)

Cholesterol: 0mg (0% Daily Value)

Sodium: 756mg (33% Daily Value)

Total Carbohydrate: 19.6g (7% Daily Value)

Dietary Fiber: 1.7g (6% Daily Value)

Total Sugars: 0.6g

Protein: 8g

Dry Cranberries Bread

Preparation Time: 20 Minutes | **Cook Time:** 25 Minutes | **Servings:** 3-4

Ingredients:

1-1/2 cups almond flour

1/4 cup melted butter

1/2 cup almond milk

1 teaspoon vanilla extract

4 tablespoons brown sugar

1/3 cup cranberries

1 teaspoon dry yeast, dissolved in 2 tablespoons of warm water

Pinch of salt

Oil spray

Directions:

In a large bowl, combine the melted butter, vanilla extract, and yeast water. Add a pinch of salt and the brown sugar to this mixture.

Gradually add the almond flour and almond milk to the mixture, stirring until you have a smooth batter. Gently fold in the cranberries into the batter.

Grease a baking pan with oil spray and spread the bread mixture evenly in the pan.

Place the pan in the air fryer and set the timer to 25 minutes at 400 degrees F or 200 degrees C.

Once the bread has finished baking and has a golden-brown crust, remove it from the air fryer.

Slice and serve your delicious almond cranberry bread. Enjoy!

Nutrition Facts:

Servings: 4

Amount per serving:

Calories: 259

Total Fat: 22.2g (28% Daily Value)

Saturated Fat: 13.9g (70% Daily Value)

Cholesterol: 31mg (10% Daily Value)

Sodium: 131mg (6% Daily Value)

Total Carbohydrate: 13.3g (5% Daily Value)

Dietary Fiber: 2g (7% Daily Value)

Total Sugars: 10.2g

Protein: 2.7g

Tapioca Cheesy Bread
Preparation Time: 12 Minutes | **Cook Time:** 15-18 Minutes | **Servings:** 2

Ingredients:

   7 ounces of Tapioca flour

   3 teaspoons baking powder

   7 ounces cheddar cheese

   7 ounces Swiss cheese

   3 large organic eggs, whisked

   1 cup heavy cream

Directions:

   In a large mixing bowl, combine the tapioca flour, baking powder, cheddar cheese, Swiss cheese, whisked eggs, and heavy cream.

   Mix the ingredients to form a dough.

   On a flat surface, knead the dough with additional tapioca flour and allow it to rest for 30 minutes.

   Line a baking pan with parchment paper.

   Preheat your air fryer to 400 degrees F (204 degrees C) or your oven to 400 degrees F (204 degrees C).

   Place the dough in the prepared pan and bake for 15-18 minutes, or until the bread is golden and cooked through.

   Once baked, let the bread cool down.

   Serve and enjoy your freshly baked cheese bread!

Nutrition Facts:

   Servings: 2

   Amount per serving:

   Calories: 1473

   Total Fat: 89.4g (115% Daily Value)

   Saturated Fat: 54.7g (273% Daily Value)

   Cholesterol: 600mg (200% Daily Value)

   Sodium: 944mg (41% Daily Value)

Total Carbohydrate: 103.6g (38% Daily Value)

Dietary Fiber: 1.2g (4% Daily Value)

Total Sugars: 1.9g

Protein: 61.7g

Cloud Bread

Preparation Time: 10 Minutes | **Cook Time:** 8 Minutes | **Servings:** 2

Ingredients:

3-4 teaspoons Cream of Tartar

4 Eggs Separated

1 cup Greek Yogurt

4 tablespoons of Stevia

Directions:

In a mixing bowl, whisk the egg whites until they form stiff peaks. Combine the stevia and cream of tartar into this mixture, gently folding them in.

In a separate small bowl, whisk the egg yolks and Greek yogurt until well blended.

Gradually add the whipped egg whites to the egg yolk and yogurt mixture, gently folding them together until fully combined.

Line a cake pan with parchment paper, ensuring it fits within your air fryer basket.

Place the prepared cake pan in the air fryer basket.

Set the air fryer to 350 degrees Fahrenheit or 170 degrees Celsius and cook for 6-8 minutes. Check periodically; the cake should become fluffy and golden.

Once the cake is cooked to perfection, remove it from the air fryer, let it cool for a moment, and then serve and enjoy!

Nutrition Facts:

Servings: 2

Amount per serving:

Calories: 229

Total Fat: 11.9g (15% Daily Value)

Saturated Fat: 4.6g (23% Daily Value)

Cholesterol: 375mg (125% Daily Value)

Sodium: 165mg (7% Daily Value)

Total Carbohydrate: 7.5g (3% Daily Value)

Dietary Fiber: 0g (0% Daily Value)

Total Sugars: 4.8g

Protein: 22.5g

Simple Milky Quick Bread

Preparation Time: 15 Minutes | **Cook Time:** 20 Minutes | **Makes:** 4 Servings

Ingredients:

1 cup all-purpose flour

1 teaspoon baking soda

1 teaspoon baking powder

1 teaspoon salt

6 tablespoons melted butter

3 eggs

1 teaspoon vanilla extract

1 cup almond milk

Directions:

In a mixing bowl, combine the all-purpose flour, baking soda, baking powder, and salt. Mix in the melted butter until the mixture is crumbly.

Add the eggs, sugar, vanilla extract, and almond milk to the dry ingredients. Stir the mixture thoroughly until it forms a smooth batter.

Grease an air fryer-safe pan with non-stick cooking spray. Pour the prepared batter into the pan, spreading it evenly.

Set your air fryer to 400 degrees F (204 degrees C) and cook for 20 minutes. Allow the bread to cool down before slicing.

Once cooled, slice and serve. Enjoy your freshly baked almond milk bread!

Nutrition Facts:

Servings: 4

Amount per serving:

Calories: 570

Total Fat: 35.5g (45% Daily Value)

Saturated Fat: 24.7g (124% Daily Value)

Cholesterol: 169mg (56% Daily Value)

Sodium: 1076mg (47% Daily Value)

Total Carbohydrate: 52g (19% Daily Value)

Dietary Fiber: 3g (11% Daily Value)

Total Sugars: 2.6g

Protein: 12.2g

Air Fryer Chocolate Chip Quick Bread

Preparation Time: 15 Minutes | **Cook Time:** 20 Minutes | **Servings:** 4

Ingredients:

1 cup all-purpose flour

1 tablespoon baking soda

1 tablespoon baking powder

A pinch of salt

6 tablespoons melted butter

2/3 cup sugar

3 eggs

1 teaspoon vanilla extract

1 cup buttermilk

1/2 cup chocolate chips

Directions:

In a mixing bowl, combine the all-purpose flour, baking soda, baking powder, salt, and melted butter.

Add the sugar, eggs, vanilla extract, and buttermilk to the dry ingredients. Mix thoroughly until you have a well-combined batter.

Grease the air fryer basket with cooking spray or a light coating of oil.

Fold in the chocolate chips into the batter for a delightful touch.

Spread the prepared batter evenly in the air fryer pan.

Set the air fryer to 350 degrees Fahrenheit (170 degrees C) and cook for 20 minutes.

Once the chocolate chip bread is done, allow it to cool before slicing.

Serve and savor your delicious homemade chocolate chip bread!

Nutrition Facts:

Servings: 4

Amount per serving:

Calories: 693

Total Fat: 28g (36% Daily Value)

Saturated Fat: 16.8g (84% Daily Value)

Cholesterol: 176mg (59% Daily Value)

Sodium: 1148mg (50% Daily Value)

Total Carbohydrate: 97.4g (35% Daily Value)

Dietary Fiber: 2.4g (9% Daily Value)

Total Sugars: 47.6g

Protein: 14.4g

Air Fryer Cinnamon Raisin Bread

Preparation Time: 25 Minutes | **Cook Time:** 12 Minutes | **Servings:** 3-4

Ingredients:

Yeast Mixture:

1 tablespoon active dry yeast

1 cup warm water

1/4 cup granulated sugar

Dough Ingredients:

1/4 cup sugar

1/8 cup olive oil

Pinch of salt

1 egg

3 cups all-purpose flour

1 cup raisins

½ tablespoon ground cinnamon

Other Ingredients:

Melted butter, as needed

Directions:

In a small mixing bowl, combine the active dry yeast, 1/4 cup granulated sugar, and warm water. Allow the yeast mixture to sit for approximately 10 minutes.

To the yeast mixture, add 1/4 cup sugar, olive oil, a pinch of salt, egg, all-purpose flour, ground cinnamon, and raisins. Mix thoroughly.

Let the dough mixture rest for about an hour, allowing it to double in size.

After the dough has risen, knead it and incorporate ground cinnamon. Then, shape the dough and place it in a greased loaf pan.

Cover the dough with a clean kitchen towel and let it sit for another hour.

Grease the loaf pan with melted butter and air fry at 350 degrees Fahrenheit or 170 degrees Celsius for 10-12 minutes until the bread is fully baked.

Once the raisin cinnamon bread is beautifully baked, serve it and savor the delicious flavors!

Nutrition Facts:

Servings: 4

Amount per serving:

Calories: 652

Total Fat: 13.4g (17% Daily Value)

Saturated Fat: 3.6g (18% Daily Value)

Cholesterol: 55mg (18% Daily Value)

Sodium: 681mg (30% Daily Value)

Total Carbohydrate: 122.3g (44% Daily Value)

Dietary Fiber: 4.5g (16% Daily Value)

Total Sugars: 38.8g

Protein: 14g

CHAPTER 9: DESSERT RECIPES

Strawberry Cupcakes with Creamy Strawberry Frosting

Preparation Time: 24 Minutes | **Cook Time:** 8 Minutes | **Servings:** 3

Ingredients:

For the Cupcakes:

 1 cup of butter

 1/2 cup of caster sugar

 2 medium eggs

 1 cup of self-rising flour

 1 teaspoon of vanilla extract

For the Topping:

 2/3 cup of butter

 2 cups of icing sugar

 2 tablespoons of whipped cream

 1 cup of blended strawberries

Directions:

Begin by preheating your air fryer to 350 degrees F or 176 degrees C.

Using a hand mixer or a beater, cream together the butter and caster sugar in a mixing bowl until well combined.

In a separate bowl, whisk the eggs and vanilla extract until they become frothy.

Gradually add a small amount of self-rising flour to the butter and sugar mixture, then fold in the remaining flour until fully incorporated. Ensure the batter is well mixed.

Fill cupcake liners with the batter and place them in the preheated air fryer.

Cook the cupcakes for 8 minutes at 350 degrees F or 176 degrees C in the air fryer until they are golden and cooked through.

While the cupcakes are baking, prepare the topping by whisking together the butter, icing sugar, whipped cream, and blended strawberries in a mixing bowl until the mixture becomes frothy and well combined.

Transfer the frosting mixture into a piping bag, filling it halfway.

Once the cupcakes are done baking, remove them from the air fryer and let them cool slightly.

Pipe the prepared frosting onto the cupcakes generously.

Your mouthwatering strawberry cupcakes are now ready to be savored.

Nutrition Facts:

Servings: 3

Amount per serving:

Calories: 1001

Total Fat: 49.3g (63% Daily Value)

Saturated Fat: 30g (150% Daily Value)

Cholesterol: 204mg (68% Daily Value)

Sodium: 360mg (16% Daily Value)

Total Carbohydrate: 132.9g (48% Daily Value)

Dietary Fiber: 1.7g (6% Daily Value)

Total Sugars: 84.3g

Protein: 9.9g

Cookie Dough

Preparation Time: 10 Minutes | **Cook Time:** 20 Minutes | **Servings:** 4

Ingredients:

1 cup of butter

5 tablespoons of brown sugar

3 cups of self-rising flour

2 cups of chocolate chips

5 tablespoons of honey

2 tablespoons of milk

2 cups of cream

Directions:

Begin by preheating your air fryer to 400 degrees F or 204 degrees C for about 5 minutes.

In a mixing bowl, whisk together the butter and brown sugar until the mixture becomes creamy.

Add the cream to the butter and sugar mixture and continue to mix.

Incorporate the honey and self-rising flour into the mixture, ensuring that all ingredients are thoroughly combined.

Sprinkle the chocolate chips over the batter and then pour in the milk.

Mix the batter until all ingredients are well incorporated.

Fill an air fryer pan halfway with the batter, ensuring it's evenly spread.

Bake in the air fryer for 20 minutes until the dessert is cooked and has a golden-brown appearance.

Your delightful dessert is now ready to be enjoyed.

Nutrition Facts:

Servings: 4

Amount per serving:

Calories: 1401

Total Fat: 78.7g (101% Daily Value)

Saturated Fat: 51g (255% Daily Value)

Cholesterol: 165mg (55% Daily Value)

Sodium: 442mg (19% Daily Value)

Total Carbohydrate: 158.3g (58% Daily Value)

Dietary Fiber: 5.4g (19% Daily Value)

Total Sugars: 78.8g

Protein: 17.9g

Flourless Shortbread Cookies

Preparation Time: 24 Minutes | **Cook Time:** 20 Minutes | **Servings:** 2-3

Ingredients:

2 cups of almond flour

1 cup of brown sugar

1 cup of butter

2 teaspoons of Vanilla Essence

Directions:

Preheat your air fryer to 350 degrees F or 176 degrees C.

In a mixing bowl, combine all the ingredients to create a soft dough resembling ice cream.

Using a cutter, shape the dough into your desired cookie shapes.

Place the shaped dough in the air fryer basket and cook for 10 minutes.

After the initial 10 minutes, carefully remove the air fryer basket and sprinkle chocolate buttons on top of the cookies.

Continue cooking for an additional 10 minutes or until all the chocolate has melted and the cookies have a golden-brown appearance.

Your delectable flourless shortbread cookies are now ready to be enjoyed.

Nutrition Facts:

Servings: 2

Amount per serving:

Calories: 1261

Total Fat: 106.1g (136% Daily Value)

Saturated Fat: 59.3g (296% Daily Value)

Cholesterol: 244mg (81% Daily Value)

Sodium: 674mg (29% Daily Value)

Total Carbohydrate: 77.7g (28% Daily Value)

Dietary Fiber: 3g (11% Daily Value)

Total Sugars: 71.9g

Protein: 7.1g

Oat Sandwich Biscuits

Preparation Time: 24 Minutes | **Cook Time:** 15 Minutes | **Servings:** 3

Ingredients:

3 cups of plain flour

1 cup of butter

1 cup of white sugar

2 beaten eggs

1/4 cup of desiccated coconut

1 cup of oats

1/2 cup of white chocolate

2 teaspoons of vanilla extract

Filling Ingredients:

1 cup of icing sugar

1/4 cup of butter

Juice of 2 small lemons

2 teaspoons of vanilla extract

Directions:

Begin by mixing the butter and white sugar in a mixing bowl until the mixture becomes light and fluffy.

In another bowl, combine the beaten eggs, desiccated coconut, oats, white chocolate, and vanilla extract. Mix these ingredients thoroughly.

Gradually add the plain flour to the mixture and continue to blend until all the ingredients are well combined.

Take the dough and roll it into medium-sized biscuit shapes. Coat each biscuit with oats for added texture.

Preheat your air fryer to 350 degrees F or 176 degrees C. Place the coated biscuits in the air fryer and cook for 15 minutes until they turn golden brown and crispy.

While the biscuits are baking, prepare the filling by mixing icing sugar, butter, lemon juice, and vanilla extract. Whisk these ingredients together until you have a smooth and creamy filling.

Once the biscuits are done and have cooled, spread the prepared filling on top of one biscuit and then sandwich it with another biscuit to create oatmeal sandwich biscuits.

Your delightful oatmeal sandwich biscuits are ready to be enjoyed. Serve and savor the deliciousness!

Nutrition Facts:

Servings: 2

Amount per serving:

Calories: 2655

Total Fat: 105.7g (135% Daily Value)

Saturated Fat: 34g (170% Daily Value)

Cholesterol: 70mg (23% Daily Value)

Sodium: 844mg (37% Daily Value)

Total Carbohydrate: 384.2g (140% Daily Value)

Dietary Fiber: 19.6g (70% Daily Value)

Total Sugars: 196.2g

Protein: 59.4g

Smarties Cookies

Preparation Time: 24 Minutes | **Cook Time:** 10 Minutes | **Servings:** 3

Ingredients:

1/3 cup of butter

1/2 cup of caster sugar

3 cups of flour

2 teaspoons of vanilla essence

6 tablespoons of milk

5 tablespoons of cocoa powder

2 ounces of Smarties

1/4 cup dark chocolate

Directions:

Begin by preheating your air fryer to 356 degrees F (180 degrees C).

In a mixing bowl, combine the cocoa powder, flour, and caster sugar. Add the butter and vanilla essence to the dry ingredients.

Mix everything thoroughly to form a well-combined dough.

Next, incorporate the chocolate chips and milk into the dough, ensuring they are evenly distributed.

Roll out the cookie dough and use a cookie cutter to create your desired biscuit shapes. Sprinkle Smarties on top of each cookie.

Place the cookies in the air fryer basket.

Cook the cookies for 10 minutes at 350 degrees F (176 degrees C) in the air fryer until they are baked to perfection.

Allow the cookies to cool before serving. Enjoy these delightful Smart Cookies as a sweet treat!

Nutrition Facts:

Servings: 3

Amount per serving:

Calories: 1319

Total Fat: 41.5g (53% Daily Value)

Saturated Fat: 25.7g (128% Daily Value)

Cholesterol: 90mg (30% Daily Value)

Sodium: 263mg (11% Daily Value)

Total Carbohydrate: 215.8g (78% Daily Value)

Dietary Fiber: 9.8g (35% Daily Value)

Total Sugars: 64.2g

Protein: 25.2g

Lemon Butterfly Buns with Cherries on Top

Preparation Time: 24 Minutes | **Cook Time:** 10 Minutes | **Servings:** 3

Ingredients:

1 cup of butter

1 cup of caster sugar

3 medium eggs

2 cups of self-raising flour

2 teaspoons of vanilla extract

Topping Ingredients:

6 teaspoons of cherries

1/2 cup of butter

2 cups of icing sugar

2 cups of cream

Directions:

Start by preheating your air fryer to 350 degrees F or 176 degrees C.

In a mixing bowl, cream together the butter and caster sugar.

Add in the eggs, vanilla extract, and flour to the same mixing bowl. Gently combine all these ingredients to create a smooth dough.

Fill 6 bun pans halfway with the prepared dough.

Cook the buns in the air fryer at 350 degrees F or 176 degrees C for 10 minutes (adjust cooking time based on your air fryer's capacity).

While the buns are cooking, prepare the topping. In a separate bowl, combine icing sugar, cream, butter, and cherries. Mix until you have a creamy icing.

Once the buns are done cooking, slice them and generously fill the center with the creamy icing sugar mixture.

Your delectable lemon butterfly buns with cherries on top are now ready to be savored.

Nutrition Facts:

Servings: 4 (Note: The servings mentioned in the original recipe were 3, but the nutrition facts are calculated for 4 servings.)

Amount per serving:

Calories: 1200

Total Fat: 57g (73% Daily Value)

Saturated Fat: 34.5g (173% Daily Value)

Cholesterol: 268mg (89% Daily Value)

Sodium: 419mg (18% Daily Value)

Total Carbohydrate: 164.5g (60% Daily Value)

Dietary Fiber: 1.8g (6% Daily Value)

Total Sugars: 111.9g

Protein: 12.2g

Empanada Wraps

Preparation Time: 20 Minutes | **Cook Time:** 10 Minutes | **Servings:** 4

Ingredients:

12 empanada wrappers, thawed

1 apple

5 tablespoons raw honey

2 teaspoons vanilla extract

1 teaspoon cinnamon

2/8 teaspoon nutmeg

4 teaspoons corn-starch

3 teaspoons water

2 eggs beaten for coating

Oil spray, for greasing

Directions:

Start by preheating your air fryer to 400 degrees F or 204 degrees C for 7 minutes, using the power button.

In a pot, cook the apple, honey, vanilla essence, cinnamon, and nutmeg for 2 minutes.

In a mixing bowl, combine corn-starch and water, then add this mixture to the sauce. Cook for an additional 1 minute. Allow the mixture to fully chill before proceeding.

Using an egg wash brush, moisten the empanada wrapper and place the apple filling over the edges.

Fold the empanadas, sealing the edges with a fork. Press the fork firmly against the edges to ensure a good seal.

Grease the basket of the air fryer with oil spray.

Place the wrapped empanadas in the air fryer basket.

Cook them for 10 minutes at 400 degrees F or 204 degrees C. Once they're done, remove, serve, and enjoy.

Nutrition Facts:

Servings: 4

Amount per serving:

Calories: 896

Total Fat: 29.9g (38% Daily Value)

Saturated Fat: 16g (80% Daily Value)

Cholesterol: 101mg (34% Daily Value)

Sodium: 1070mg (47% Daily Value)

Total Carbohydrate: 144.5g (53% Daily Value)

Dietary Fiber: 8.3g (30% Daily Value)

Total Sugars: 55.6g

Protein: 15.4g

Mini Strawberry and Cream Pies

Preparation Time: 12 Minutes | **Cook Time:** 12 Minutes | **Servings:** 4

Ingredients:

2 boxes of Store-Bought Pie Dough

2 cups of cubed strawberries

4 tablespoons of heavy cream

3 tablespoons of almonds

2 egg whites (for brushing)

Directions:

Start by flattening out the pie dough on a clean, level surface. Using a circular cutter, cut the dough into 4-inch circles.

Brush the edges of each dough circle with egg white. Then, place another circle on top and press the edges together using a fork to seal them.

In the center of each dough circle, evenly distribute the almonds, strawberries, and drizzle with heavy cream.

Arrange the prepared mini pies on a baking pan and place it inside the basket of the air fryer.

Set the air fryer to 400 degrees F or 204 degrees C and cook for 12 minutes until the pies turn golden brown and the filling is bubbling.

Once they are done cooking, remove the Mini Strawberry and Cream Pies from the air fryer and let them cool slightly.

Serve these delightful pies and savor every bite.

Nutrition Facts:

Servings: 4

Amount per serving:

Calories: 350

Total Fat: 20.5g (26% Daily Value)

Saturated Fat: 9.7g (48% Daily Value)

Cholesterol: 26mg (9% Daily Value)

Sodium: 185mg (8% Daily Value)

Total Carbohydrate: 38.1g (14% Daily Value)

Dietary Fiber: 3.4g (12% Daily Value)

Total Sugars: 24.9g

Protein: 6.1g

Ginger Cranberry Scones
Preparation Time: 24 Minutes | **Cook Time:** 15 Minutes | **Servings:** 3-4

Ingredients:

3 cups all-purpose flour

1/6 cup dark brown sugar

1 teaspoon Baking Powder

1 teaspoon cinnamon

2 teaspoons freshly ground nutmeg

2 teaspoons cloves

2 teaspoons salt

Pinch of ginger powder

2 cups dried cranberries

14 tablespoons unsalted butter, frozen, grated on a box grater

2/3 cup heavy cream, plus more for glazing

2 teaspoons Canola Oil

2 large eggs

2 teaspoons Vanilla Extract

2 cups sour cream

Demerara sugar, for sprinkling

Directions:

Begin by preheating your air fryer to 350 degrees F or 176 degrees C.

In a large mixing bowl, combine the flour, dark brown sugar, baking powder, cinnamon, nutmeg, cloves, salt, ginger powder, and dried cranberries.

Add the grated frozen butter to the dry ingredients and mix well.

In a separate bowl, whisk together the heavy cream, eggs, vanilla extract, and sour cream until well combined.

Combine the wet and dry ingredients in a mixing bowl to form the scone dough.

Shape the dough into a 3/4-inch thick circle and cut it into 8 wedges.

Brush the top of each wedge with canola oil and sprinkle Demerara sugar over them.

Place the scones in the air fryer basket and cook for 15 minutes, making sure to rotate them halfway through for even cooking.

Once the scones are golden brown and cooked through, remove them from the air fryer.

Serve the Ginger Cranberry Scones and enjoy your delicious treat.

Nutrition Facts:

Servings: 4

Amount per serving:

Calories: 1140

Total Fat: 78.2g (100% Daily Value)

Saturated Fat: 46.6g (233% Daily Value)

Cholesterol: 278mg (93% Daily Value)

Sodium: 1560mg (68% Daily Value)

Total Carbohydrate: 90.7g (33% Daily Value)

Dietary Fiber: 5.5g (20% Daily Value)

Total Sugars: 9.1g

Protein: 17.5g

Air Fryer Baked Apples

Preparation Time: 18 Minutes | **Cook Time:** 8 Minutes | **Servings:** 3

Ingredients:

2 Apples

1 teaspoon cinnamon

Salt (to taste)

Topping Ingredients:

2 tablespoons melted butter

2 tablespoons Maple syrup

1 teaspoon Cinnamon

Directions:

Begin by preheating your air fryer to 400 degrees F.

In a bowl, combine the cinnamon and a pinch of salt.

Slice the apples and generously sprinkle them with the cinnamon-salt mixture.

Arrange the apple slices in the air fryer basket.

Bake the apple slices in the air fryer for 6-8 minutes, making sure to toss them halfway through the cooking time for even browning.

Once the apple slices are tender and lightly caramelized, transfer them to a serving plate.

For the topping, mix the melted butter, maple syrup, and the remaining teaspoon of cinnamon.

Drizzle the luscious topping over the baked apple slices.

Serve your cinnamon-spiced apple slices while they are warm and fragrant.

Nutrition Facts:

Servings: 3

Amount per serving:

Calories: 222

Total Fat: 8.1g (10% Daily Value)

Saturated Fat: 4.9g (24% Daily Value)

Cholesterol: 20mg (7% Daily Value)

Sodium: 58mg (3% Daily Value)

Total Carbohydrate: 41g (15% Daily Value)

Dietary Fiber: 6.2g (22% Daily Value)

Total Sugars: 31.2g

Protein: 0.7g

Grill Peaches

Preparation Time: 10 Minutes | **Cook Time:** 5 Minutes | **Makes:** 2 Servings

Ingredients:

1 yellow peach

1/4 cup graham cracker crumbs

1/4 cup brown sugar

1/4 cup cubed butter

Whipped Cream (as needed)

Directions:

Start by cleaning the peach and cutting it into wedges.

Line the air fryer basket with parchment paper. Arrange the peach wedges on the parchment paper in the air fryer.

Bake the peaches in the air fryer at 350 degrees F or 176 degrees C for 5 minutes. Ensure the skin side of the peaches is facing down during baking.

While the peaches are baking, mix the graham cracker crumbs, brown sugar, and cubed butter in a bowl until well combined.

Once the peaches have finished baking, remove them from the air fryer. Keep the skin side down and generously sprinkle the crumb mixture over the top of the peaches.

Serve your delicious graham cracker crumb-topped peach wedges immediately. You can also add a dollop of whipped cream for an extra treat.

Nutrition Facts:

Servings: 2

Amount per serving:

Calories: 728

Total Fat: 61g (78% Daily Value)

Saturated Fat: 37.7g (188% Daily Value)

Cholesterol: 194mg (65% Daily Value)

Sodium: 312mg (14% Daily Value)

Total Carbohydrate: 42g (15% Daily Value)

Dietary Fiber: 0.7g (2% Daily Value)

Total Sugars: 29.7g

Protein: 3.5g

Air fryer Cookies

Preparation Time: 15 minutes | **Cook Time:** 10 minutes | **Servings:** 3

Ingredients:

1/6 cup melted butter

1 cup caster sugar

3 cups self-rising flour

1 teaspoon vanilla essence

8 tablespoons coconut milk

1 cup cocoa powder

Oil spray

Directions:

Begin by preheating your air fryer to 350 degrees F or 176 degrees C.

In a mixing bowl, combine the cocoa powder and self-rising flour, ensuring they are well-mixed.

In a separate bowl, whisk together the melted butter, caster sugar, vanilla essence, and coconut milk until you have a smooth mixture.

Now, combine the wet and dry ingredients to form a dough. Mix thoroughly until everything is well incorporated.

Roll out the cookie dough and use a cookie cutter to shape the cookies. Place them on a baking sheet lined with parchment paper.

Carefully transfer the baking sheet with the cookies into the preheated air fryer.

Cook the cookies in the air fryer for 10 minutes at 350 degrees F or 176 degrees C. Keep an eye on them to ensure they don't overcook.

Once they are done and have a delightful golden-brown color, remove the cookies from the air fryer, allow them to cool, and then serve and enjoy your homemade cocoa cookies!

Nutrition Facts:

Servings: 3

Amount per serving:

Calories: 957

Total Fat: 25g (32% Daily Value)

Saturated Fat: 17.4g (87% Daily Value)

Cholesterol: 27mg (9% Daily Value)

Sodium: 87mg (4% Daily Value)

Total Carbohydrate: 180.2g (66% Daily Value)

Dietary Fiber: 12.8g (46% Daily Value)

Total Sugars: 69g

Protein: 19.1g

Oat Sandwich Biscuits

Preparation Time: 12 Minutes | **Cook Time:** 15 Minutes | **Servings:** 3

Ingredients:

3 cups plain flour

1/4 cup butter

1/4 cup white sugar

2 eggs

1 cup desiccated coconut

2 cups oats

2 cups white chocolate

2 teaspoons vanilla extract

Directions:

In a mixing bowl, combine the butter and sugar using either a hand mixer or a food processor until well blended.

Beat the eggs and add them to the mixture. Then incorporate the desiccated coconut, oats, white chocolate, and vanilla extract into the mixture.

Gradually add the plain flour to the prepared mixture and mix until a dough forms.

Grease the air fryer basket with cooking spray to prevent sticking.

Shape the dough into biscuits or cookies of your desired size and place them in the greased air fryer basket.

Set the air fryer to 350 degrees F or 176 degrees C and cook for 15 minutes. Ensure the biscuits are evenly cooked and have a golden hue.

Once the biscuits are baked to perfection, remove them from the air fryer and let them cool slightly before serving. Enjoy your homemade coconut and white chocolate oat biscuits!

Nutrition Facts:

Servings: 3

Amount per serving:

Calories: 1957

Total Fat: 102g (131% Daily Value)

Saturated Fat: 71.2g (356% Daily Value)

Cholesterol: 174mg (58% Daily Value)

Sodium: 283mg (12% Daily Value)

Total Carbohydrate: 232.3g (84% Daily Value)

Dietary Fiber: 19.9g (71% Daily Value)

Total Sugars: 89.9g

Protein: 35.1g

Fryer Keto Brownies
Preparation Time: 10 Minutes | **Cook Time:** 10 Minutes | **Servings:** 4

Ingredients:

1/2 cup Almond Flour

5 tablespoons Sweetener

1/4 teaspoon Baking Powder

5 tablespoons Unsweetened Cocoa Powder

3 Eggs

6 tablespoons melted butter

4 tablespoons chocolate chips

4 chopped pecans

Directions:

Start by preheating your air fryer to 350 degrees F or 176 degrees C.

In a mixing bowl, whisk together the almond flour, baking powder, cocoa powder, and sweetener until well combined.

Combine the eggs and melted butter with the dry ingredients, stirring until you achieve a smooth consistency.

Add the chopped pecans and chocolate chips to the mixture, gently folding them in.

Grease the ramekins, then pour the brownie mixture evenly into each one.

Place the ramekins in the preheated air fryer and bake for 10 minutes.

Once the brownies are done, allow them to cool for a bit before serving.

Nutrition Facts:

Servings: 4

Amount per serving:

Calories: 389

Total Fat: 36.3g (47% Daily Value)

Saturated Fat: 15.8g (79% Daily Value)

Cholesterol: 171mg (57% Daily Value)

Sodium: 179mg (8% Daily Value)

Total Carbohydrate: 13.1g (5% Daily Value)

Dietary Fiber: 4.5g (16% Daily Value)

Total Sugars: 6.4g

Protein: 8.7g

Peanut Butter Cupcake

Preparation Time: 10 Minutes | **Cook Time:** 16 Minutes | **Servings:** 3

Ingredients:

1-1/2 cups all-purpose flour

1/3 cup cocoa powder

1/2 teaspoon baking powder

1/2 teaspoon baking soda

Salt (to taste)

3 eggs

1/2 cup brown sugar

1/2 cup Almond oil

1 teaspoon pure vanilla extract

1/2 cup almond milk

Directions:

Begin by whisking the eggs and brown sugar together in a large mixing bowl until fully combined.

Once the egg-sugar mixture is thoroughly mixed, add the almond milk and pure vanilla extract to it. Continue to mix until all the liquid ingredients are well incorporated.

In a separate mixing bowl, combine the dry ingredients, including all-purpose flour, cocoa powder, baking powder, baking soda, and a pinch of salt. Mix these dry ingredients thoroughly.

Now, combine the wet and dry ingredients, blending them together until you have a smooth batter.

Pour the cupcake batter into muffin cups, filling them evenly.

Place the muffin cups in your air fryer and cook for approximately 14-16 minutes at 350 degrees F or 176 degrees C. Ensure they are fully cooked by inserting a toothpick into a cupcake; it should come out clean when they are done.

Once baked to perfection, remove the cupcakes from the air fryer, allow them to cool slightly, and then serve.

Nutrition Facts:

Servings: 3

Amount per serving:

Calories: 746

Total Fat: 51.9g (67% Daily Value)

Saturated Fat: 13.6g (68% Daily Value)

Cholesterol: 164mg (55% Daily Value)

Sodium: 289mg (13% Daily Value)

Total Carbohydrate: 63.9g (23% Daily Value)

Dietary Fiber: 4.9g (17% Daily Value)

Total Sugars: 25.6g

Protein: 12.5g

Orange Cornmeal Cake

Preparation Time: 10 Minutes | **Cook Time:** 25 Minutes | **Servings:** 3

Ingredients:

1 cup all-purpose flour

1 cup yellow cornmeal

1 cup white sugar

1 teaspoon baking soda

1/2 cup olive oil

1 cup orange juice

1 teaspoon vanilla

1/2 cup powdered sugar

Oil spray

Directions:

Begin by greasing the baking pan with oil and setting it aside for later use.

In a mixing bowl, combine all the ingredients one by one, ensuring that you achieve a smooth batter consistency.

Once the batter is ready, transfer it into the prepared baking pan.

Preheat your air fryer to 350 degrees F or 176 degrees C.

Place the filled baking pan into the air fryer and cook for 25 minutes. Make sure to check for doneness with a toothpick; it should come out clean when inserted into the center of the cake.

Once the cake has finished cooking and is cooled enough, you can serve and enjoy this delightful cornbread cake.

Nutrition Facts:

Servings: 3

Amount per serving:

Calories: 1109

Total Fat: 36.3g (46% Daily Value)

Saturated Fat: 5.2g (26% Daily Value)

Cholesterol: 0mg (0% Daily Value)

Sodium: 436mg (19% Daily Value)

Total Carbohydrate: 190.2g (69% Daily Value)

Dietary Fiber: 5.4g (19% Daily Value)

Total Sugars: 93.8g

Protein: 12.5g

CHAPTER 10: AIR FRYER RECIPES FOR ONE

Tandoori Paneer Naan Pizza

Preparation Time: 20 Minutes | **Cook Time:** 10 Minutes | **Servings:** 1

Ingredients:

2 Garlic Naan

1/4 cup Pizza sauce or Marinara sauce

1/4 cup Grape Tomatoes, cut into halves

1/4 cup Red Onions, sliced

1/4 cup Bell Pepper, sliced

3/4 cup Mozzarella, grated

2 tablespoons Feta (optional)

2 tablespoons Cilantro, chopped

For Tandoori Paneer:

1/2 cup Paneer, small cubes

1 tablespoon Yogurt, thick

1/2 teaspoon Garam Masala

1/2 teaspoon Garlic Powder

1/4 teaspoon Ground Turmeric (Haldi Powder)

1/2 teaspoon Kashmiri Red Chili Powder or mild paprika (adjust to taste)

1/4 teaspoon Salt (adjust to taste)

Directions:

In a bowl, combine all the ingredients listed for Tandoori Paneer.

Line a baking tray with parchment paper. Place the Garlic Naan on the baking tray and evenly spread pizza sauce on each naan. Sprinkle a portion of mozzarella over both naans.

Add the marinated paneer cubes (mixed with yogurt and spices) onto the naans. Follow by arranging the red onions, bell peppers, and grape tomatoes on top.

Cover the veggies with an even layer of mozzarella. If desired, sprinkle some feta cheese on top. Finish by adding chopped cilantro.

If using an air fryer, cook at 400 degrees F or 204 degrees C for 8-10 minutes. Begin checking after 7 minutes and cook to your preferred level of crispiness.

Garnish with chili flakes and savor your delicious Garlic Naan Pizza!

Nutrition Facts:

Servings: 1

Amount per serving:

Calories: 462

Total Fat: 9.4g (12% Daily Value)

Saturated Fat: 5.2g (26% Daily Value)

Cholesterol: 28mg (9% Daily Value)

Sodium: 1372mg (60% Daily Value)

Total Carbohydrate: 74.2g (27% Daily Value)

Dietary Fiber: 4.2g (15% Daily Value)

Total Sugars: 6.4g

Protein: 22.5g

Pumpkin Bread Pudding

Preparation Time: 20 Minutes | **Cook Time:** 40 Minutes | **Servings:** 1

Ingredients:

For Pudding:

¾ cup heavy cream

1/3 cup whole milk

½ cup canned pumpkin puree

2 tablespoons sugar

1 large egg

1 egg yolk

½ teaspoon pumpkin pie spice

1/8 teaspoon salt

4 cups day-old baguette, cubed

4 tablespoons unsalted butter, melted

For Sauce:

¼ cup heavy cream

¼ cup pure maple syrup

1 tablespoon unsalted butter

½ teaspoon vanilla extract

Directions:

Prepare the Pudding: In a mixing bowl, combine the heavy cream, whole milk, canned pumpkin puree, sugar, egg, egg yolk, pumpkin pie spice, and salt. Beat the mixture until it's well combined.

In another large bowl, place the cubed day-old baguette. Drizzle the melted butter over the bread cubes and toss them to ensure they are evenly coated.

Gently add the prepared pumpkin mixture to the bread cubes, making sure all the cubes are coated.

Transfer the mixture to an ungreased 6-inch round baking pan.

Preheat the Air Fryer: Place the "Crisper Basket" in the air fryer and set the temperature to 350 degrees F or 176 degrees C. Press "Start/Stop" to initiate the preheating process.

Cook the Pudding: When the display shows "Add Food," open the lid and carefully place the baking pan with the pudding mixture into the "Crisper Basket." Close the lid and set the cooking time for 40 minutes.

Press "Start/Stop" to start cooking.

Nutrition Facts:

Servings: 1

Amount per serving:

Calories: 1978

Total Fat: 156.2g (200% Daily Value)

Saturated Fat: 96.9g (484% Daily Value)

Cholesterol: 849mg (283% Daily Value)

Sodium: 1139mg (50% Daily Value)

Total Carbohydrate: 128.8g (47% Daily Value)

Dietary Fiber: 4.7g (17% Daily Value)

Total Sugars: 85.2g

Protein: 19.3g

Tasty Jumbo Stuffed Mushrooms

Preparation Time: 20 Minutes | **Cook Time:** 10 Minutes | **Servings:** 1

Ingredients:

6 jumbo Portobello mushrooms

1 tablespoon olive oil

1/4 cup ricotta cheese

6 tablespoons Parmesan cheese, divided

1/2 cup frozen chopped spinach, thawed and drained

1/3 cup bread crumbs

1/4 teaspoon minced fresh rosemary

Directions:

Start by wiping the Portobello mushrooms clean with a damp cloth. Remove and discard the stems. Coat the mushrooms evenly with olive oil.

Insert the Crisper Basket, close the hood, and select the AIR CRISP function. Set the temperature to 350°F and the time to 3 minutes for preheating. Bake the mushrooms for 3 minutes.

Carefully remove the mushroom caps.

In a medium-sized bowl, combine the ricotta cheese, 3 tablespoons of Parmesan cheese, chopped spinach, bread crumbs, and minced rosemary. Mix these ingredients thoroughly.

Stuff the mushroom caps with the ricotta and spinach mixture. Sprinkle the remaining Parmesan cheese on top.

Place the stuffed mushroom caps back into the basket.

Continue baking for 6 minutes at 400 degrees F or 204 degrees C or until the filling is hot and the mushrooms are nicely cooked.

Once done, remove from the air fryer, and it's time to enjoy your delicious stuffed Portobello mushrooms!

Nutrition Facts:

Servings: 1

Amount per serving:

Calories: 652

Total Fat: 32.9g (42% Daily Value)

Saturated Fat: 13.5g (68% Daily Value)

Cholesterol: 59mg (20% Daily Value)

Sodium: 873mg (38% Daily Value)

Total Carbohydrate: 49.8g (18% Daily Value)

Dietary Fiber: 8.1g (29% Daily Value)

Total Sugars: 2.5g

Protein: 48.3g

Hearty Meatball Soup

Preparation Time: 20 Minutes | **Cook Time:** 28-30 Minutes | **Servings:** 1

Ingredients: *Meatball Ingredients:*

- 1 pound ground turkey (about 500g)
- 1/4 cup finely chopped yellow onion
- 1/2 cup Panko breadcrumbs
- 1/2 tablespoon Italian seasoning
- 2 tablespoons grated Parmesan cheese
- 1 tablespoon soy sauce
- 2 teaspoons corn starch
- 1 teaspoon garlic powder
- 1 teaspoon onion powder
- 1/4 teaspoon black pepper (or to taste)

Soup Ingredients:

- 2 tablespoons olive oil
- 1 stalk celery, diced
- 2 tablespoons chopped garlic
- 1/4 cup diced yellow onion
- 1/4 cup tomato ketchup
- 1/2 cup diced carrot
- 1 large zucchini, diced
- 1/4 cup wine (rice wine recommended)
- 1 can crushed tomatoes
- 1/2 can corn kernels
- 2 cups broth (chicken broth recommended)
- 1 tablespoon Italian seasoning
- 2 teaspoons garlic powder
- Salt and pepper to taste

Directions:

Line the air fryer basket with a grill mat or lightly greased aluminum foil.

In a large mixing bowl, combine all the meatball ingredients. Take about 1 tablespoon of the mixture and roll it into a ball. Place the meatballs into the air fryer basket.

Spritz the meatballs with oil and air fry at 380 degrees F or 190 degrees C for approximately 8 minutes, shaking the basket once during cooking.

Meanwhile, in a pot, heat olive oil and sauté garlic, celery, and onion until fragrant. Add in the remaining soup ingredients and bring the mixture to a boil.

When the meatballs are done, transfer them to the pot.

Fill the pot with water just enough to cover all the ingredients. Let it simmer for about 20 minutes, allowing the flavors to meld together.

Serve the turkey meatball soup on its own or with pasta or bread.

Nutrition Facts:

Servings: 1

Amount per serving:

Calories: 1027

Total Fat: 28.5g (37% Daily Value)

Saturated Fat: 9.1g (45% Daily Value)

Cholesterol: 352mg (117% Daily Value)

Sodium: 2838mg (123% Daily Value)

Total Carbohydrate: 43.1g (16% Daily Value)

Dietary Fiber: 3g (11% Daily Value)

Total Sugars: 19.4g

Protein: 145.3g

Air Fryer Roasted Red Pepper Soup

Preparation Time: 20 Minutes | **Cook Time:** 50 Minutes | **Servings:** 1

Ingredients:

1 red bell pepper, seeds removed and quartered

2 tablespoons olive oil, divided

Salt and black pepper, to taste

2 tablespoons butter

1 large yellow onion, diced

2 garlic cloves, minced

1/4 teaspoon dried basil

1/4 teaspoon dried oregano

1 1/2 cups chicken or vegetable broth

1/4 teaspoon soy sauce

1/2 cup half & half

1/4 teaspoon onion powder

1/2 teaspoon garlic powder

A dash of Worcestershire sauce

Directions:

Start by preheating your air fryer to 400 degrees F or 204 degrees C.

Toss the red bell peppers with 1 tablespoon of olive oil, salt, and black pepper to taste. Place the seasoned peppers into the air fryer basket and roast for 15 minutes until they are nicely charred and tender.

While the peppers are roasting, in a medium pot over medium-high heat, heat the remaining 1 tablespoon of olive oil and the butter.

Add the diced yellow onion and cook for about 7 minutes, or until the onion turns translucent. Stir in the minced garlic and cook for an additional 1 minute until it becomes fragrant.

After roasting, add the red peppers to the pot along with dried basil, dried oregano, chicken or vegetable broth, and soy sauce. Stir everything together.

Bring the mixture to a boil, then reduce the heat to a simmer, cover the pot, and allow it to simmer for 20 minutes.

Use an immersion blender to blend the soup until it reaches a smooth and creamy consistency.

Stir in the half & half, and let the soup simmer for an additional 5 minutes.

Once ready, serve the creamy roasted red pepper soup hot, optionally garnished with a dash of Worcestershire sauce for extra flavor.

Nutrition Facts:

Servings: 1

Amount per serving:

Calories: 1073

Total Fat: 72.2g (93% Daily Value)

Saturated Fat: 29.1g (145% Daily Value)

Cholesterol: 268mg (89% Daily Value)

Sodium: 441mg (19% Daily Value)

Total Carbohydrate: 41.3g (15% Daily Value)

Dietary Fiber: 6.9g (25% Daily Value)

Total Sugars: 19.4g

Protein: 69.6g

The Best Tomato Basil Soup

Preparation Time: 20 Minutes | **Cook Time:** 30 Minutes | **Servings:** 1

Ingredients:

Oil for spraying

½ pound of red tomatoes, cut in half

1 medium red bell pepper, quartered

1 large yellow onion, quartered

1 medium carrot, chopped into large pieces

2 garlic cloves, peeled

1.5 cups chicken broth

½ cup heavy cream

4 fresh basil leaves, finely chopped

Splash of balsamic vinegar

Grated Parmesan Cheese (optional)

Directions:

Start by spraying the bottom of the air fryer basket with a light coating of oil to prevent sticking.

Add the halved red tomatoes, quartered red bell pepper, quartered yellow onion, chopped carrot, and peeled garlic cloves to the air fryer. Set the air fryer to 350 degrees F (176 degrees C) and roast the vegetables for 25 minutes.

About halfway through the roasting time, check the air fryer basket and shake it to ensure even roasting. Give it another shake when there are approximately 5 minutes left on the timer.

Once the timer goes off, transfer the roasted vegetables to a medium stockpot and add the chicken broth. Allow the mixture to come to a boil. Reduce the heat and simmer for about 5 minutes.

After simmering, use an immersion blender to blend the soup until it reaches a smooth consistency. Alternatively, let the soup cool slightly and use a traditional blender for this step.

Stir in the finely chopped basil, heavy cream, and a splash of balsamic vinegar. Season with salt and pepper to taste.

If desired, top the creamy tomato soup with grated Parmesan cheese.

Nutrition Facts:

Servings: 1

Amount per serving:

Calories: 325

Total Fat: 26g (33% Daily Value)

Saturated Fat: 15.3g (77% Daily Value)

Cholesterol: 86mg (29% Daily Value)

Sodium: 1234mg (54% Daily Value)

Total Carbohydrate: 12.1g (4% Daily Value)

Dietary Fiber: 2.7g (10% Daily Value)

Total Sugars: 7.1g

Protein: 12.4g

Air Fryer Potato Leek Cakes

Preparation Time: 15 Minutes | **Cook Time:** 10-20 Minutes | **Servings:** 1

Ingredients:

2 medium russet potatoes, peeled and diced to 1/4 inch

1 medium leek, white part only, stem removed, washed, and diced to 1/4 inch

1 medium garlic clove, minced

4 tablespoons butter

2 1/2 tablespoons kosher salt

1/2 teaspoon ground black pepper

3/4 cup heavy cream

1/4 cup Panko bread crumbs

1 egg white, beaten until frothy

1 tablespoon parsley, minced

Directions:

Begin by placing the diced potatoes, leeks, and minced garlic in a large pot. Cover them with water and bring the mixture to a boil. Cook until the potatoes are fork-tender, which should take approximately 8 to 10 minutes. Drain the mixture and transfer it to a large bowl.

Add the butter, kosher salt, black pepper, and heavy cream to the potato and leek mixture. Mash everything together using a potato masher or a large spoon until you achieve the consistency of mashed potatoes with small chunks.

Now, incorporate the Panko bread crumbs, beaten egg white, and minced parsley into the mixture. Stir until all the ingredients are thoroughly combined. Allow the mixture to cool in the refrigerator for 5 to 10 minutes.

Slightly dampen your hands and shape about 1/3 cup of the potato mixture into a patty that is approximately 2 inches wide and 1/2 inch thick. Place the formed patty on wax or parchment paper and repeat this process with the remaining mixture.

Arrange a single layer of potato cakes in the basket of your air fryer and cook them at 350°F for 10 minutes. Carefully remove them and set them aside. Repeat this step until all the cakes have been cooked.

Nutrition Facts:

Servings: 1

Amount per serving:

Calories: 1240

Total Fat: 95.3g (122% Daily Value)

Saturated Fat: 58.8g (294% Daily Value)

Cholesterol: 308mg (103% Daily Value)

Sodium: 461mg (20% Daily Value)

Total Carbohydrate: 85.8g (31% Daily Value)

Dietary Fiber: 12g (43% Daily Value)

Total Sugars: 8.8g

Protein: 14.7g

Cornmeal Fried Leek Rings

Preparation Time: 10 Minutes | **Cook Time:** 5 Minutes | **Servings:** 1

Ingredients:

4 small to medium leeks, cut into rings

1 cup buttermilk

¾ cup all-purpose flour

⅛ Stone ground cornmeal (any color)

Oil spray (for greasing)

Kosher salt and freshly ground black pepper

Directions:

Begin by removing the dark green parts of the leeks, setting them aside for compost. Slice the leeks into rings without separating them.

Place the leek rings in a bowl of water to remove any dirt (it should sink to the bottom). Submerge the leeks in buttermilk for 10 to 15 minutes.

In a mixing bowl, combine the flour, cornmeal, and season with salt and pepper to taste.

Preheat your air fryer to 350 degrees F or 176 degrees C.

Dredge the soaked leek rings in the flour mixture, ensuring they are well coated, and then lightly mist them with oil spray. Avoid overcrowding the air fryer basket.

Cook the leek rings in the air fryer for 5 minutes or until they turn a delightful golden brown.

Nutrition Facts:

Servings: 1

Amount per serving:

Calories: 513

Total Fat: 5.3g (7% Daily Value)

Saturated Fat: 2.5g (13% Daily Value)

Cholesterol: 10mg (3% Daily Value)

Sodium: 1105mg (48% Daily Value)

Total Carbohydrate: 94.7g (34% Daily Value)

Dietary Fiber: 3.6g (13% Daily Value)

Total Sugars: 14g

Protein: 19.9g

Meatloaf Sliders

Preparation Time: 18 Minutes | **Cook Time:** 15 Minutes | **Servings:** 1

Ingredients:

1 pound ground beef

1 small organic egg

1/2 tablespoon tomato paste

1/2 teaspoon Worcestershire sauce

Salt (to taste)

1/2 tablespoon brown sugar

1 green chili, chopped

1/4 cup almond flour

2 tablespoons white onion, chopped

Oil spray (for greasing)

2 slices cheddar cheese

2 large tomatoes, sliced

2 slider buns

Directions:

Preheat your air fryer to 400 degrees F or 204 degrees C for 5 minutes.

In a bowl, combine all the burger ingredients, including ground beef, organic egg, tomato paste, Worcestershire sauce, salt, brown sugar, green chili, almond flour, and chopped white onion. Mix thoroughly and form the mixture into burger patties as needed.

Grease the air fryer basket with oil spray and place the burger patties inside.

Set the air fryer to cook for 12 minutes, making sure to flip the patties halfway through the cooking time.

After the initial 12 minutes, remove the patties and top each one with cheddar cheese slices and tomato slices.

Return the patties to the air fryer and cook for an additional 4 minutes until the cheese melts, and the burgers are cooked to your desired level.

Place each burger patty on a slider bun and serve while hot.

Nutrition Facts:

Servings: 1

Amount per serving:

    Calories: 935

    Total Fat: 32.6g (42% Daily Value)

    Saturated Fat: 11.9g (60% Daily Value)

    Cholesterol: 543mg (181% Daily Value)

    Sodium: 543mg (24% Daily Value)

    Total Carbohydrate: 8.6g (3% Daily Value)

    Dietary Fiber: 0.8g (3% Daily Value)

    Total Sugars: 7g

    Protein: 142.8g

CHAPTER 11: AIR FRYER FOR TWO

Air Fryer Pork Chops with Mustard Chimichurri Sauce

Preparation Time: 15 Minutes | **Cook Time:** 20 Minutes | **Servings:** 2

Ingredients:

1 bone-in pork chop (1 1/4" to 1 1/2" thick, about 1 lb each)

1 tablespoon of kosher salt

1 tablespoon of black pepper

1 tablespoon of melted butter or olive oil

For the Mustard Chimichurri Sauce:

1/2 cup olive oil

1 tablespoon of lime juice

1 tablespoon of whole-grain Dijon mustard

1 tablespoon of honey

1 tablespoon of fresh parsley (finely chopped)

1 tablespoon of fresh cilantro (finely chopped)

1 tablespoon of red onion (finely chopped)

1 clove garlic (pressed)

1/2 tablespoon of kosher salt (plus more to taste)

1/4 tablespoon of black pepper (plus more to taste)

Instructions:

For the Mustard Chimichurri Sauce:

In a small bowl, combine olive oil, lime juice, whole-grain Dijon mustard, honey, finely chopped parsley, cilantro, red onion, pressed garlic, kosher salt, and black pepper. Mix well and refrigerate until you're ready to serve.

For the Pork Chops:

Pat the bone-in pork chop dry with paper towels.

Make small cuts along the fatty edge of the pork chop, spacing them about 1-2 inches apart. Season both sides of the chop with kosher salt and black pepper.

Transfer the seasoned pork chop to a plate and refrigerate it uncovered for a few hours or overnight to allow the flavors to meld.

Straight from the refrigerator, place the pork chop on the air fryer rack and brush it with melted butter or olive oil.

Cook the pork chop in the air fryer at 400 degrees F or 204 degrees C for approximately 20 minutes, or until the internal temperature reaches 140F. There's no need to flip or rotate it during cooking.

Once done, remove the pork chop from the air fryer and allow it to rest for 5 minutes.

Serve the cooked pork chop with the prepared chimichurri sauce and your favorite side dish.

Nutrition Facts:

Servings: 2

Amount per serving:

Calories: 784

Total Fat: 76.2g (98% Daily Value)

Saturated Fat: 18.3g (92% Daily Value)

Cholesterol: 84mg (28% Daily Value)

Sodium: 3589mg (156% Daily Value)

Total Carbohydrate: 11.8g (4% Daily Value)

Dietary Fiber: 1.1g (4% Daily Value)

Total Sugars: 8.9g

Protein: 18.7g

Crispy Air Fryer Okra with Creole Seasoning

Preparation Time: 15 Minutes | **Cook Time:** 16-20 Minutes | **Servings:** 2

Ingredients:

For the Okra:

1/2 pound of fresh okra

1/2 cup of whole milk

1/2 cup of all-purpose flour

1/2 teaspoon of paprika

1/2 teaspoon of dried thyme

1/2 teaspoon of kosher salt

1/4 teaspoon of garlic granules

1/4 teaspoon of onion granules

1/4 teaspoon of dried oregano

1/4 teaspoon of freshly ground black pepper

Pinch of ground white pepper

Pinch of cayenne

Non-stick cooking spray

For the Sauce:

1/2 cup of mayonnaise

1 tablespoon of hot sauce

1/2 the zest of a small lemon

1 teaspoon of lemon juice

Instructions:

Begin by preparing the okra. Slice off the tops (stem ends) of the okra pods and then slice them in half lengthwise, creating two long okra halves from each pod. Place these in a medium bowl and pour in the milk. Toss the okra in the milk to coat evenly.

In a large bowl, combine the flour, paprika, dried thyme, kosher salt, garlic granules, onion granules, dried oregano, black pepper, white pepper, and cayenne. Whisk these dry ingredients together.

Preheat your air fryer to 400 degrees F or 204 degrees C and set the timer for 15 minutes.

Drain any excess milk from the okra and toss the okra pieces in the flour and spice mix to ensure even coating. The okra should appear dry and thoroughly coated.

Place the individual coated okra pieces flat on a cutting board, shaking off any excess flour back into the bowl.

Spray each piece with cooking spray until the flour on the okra appears slightly wet.

Remove the air fryer tray from the air fryer and place the okra pieces sprayed-side down in the tray. Make sure they are not overlapping (you may need to work in two batches).

Spray the other side of the okra with cooking spray.

Put the tray in the air fryer and cook the okra until it becomes golden brown and crunchy, approximately 8 minutes. Ensure that no parts of the okra look dry or ashy. About halfway through the cooking time, gently shake and toss the okra, then spray them again with cooking spray.

While the okra is cooking, prepare the sauce by stirring together the mayonnaise, hot sauce, lemon zest, and lemon juice in a small bowl.

Serve the hot and crispy okra with the sauce on the side.

Nutrition Facts:

Servings: 2

Amount per serving:

Calories: 430

Total Fat: 22.3g (29% Daily Value)

Saturated Fat: 4.2g (21% Daily Value)

Cholesterol: 21mg (7% Daily Value)

Sodium: 1223mg (53% Daily Value)

Total Carbohydrate: 50.2g (18% Daily Value)

Dietary Fiber: 5g (18% Daily Value)

Total Sugars: 8.9g

Protein: 8.1g

Air Fryer Coconut, Caramel, Peanut Butter S'mores
Preparation Time: 15 Minutes | **Cook Time:** 6-8 Minutes | **Servings:** 2

Ingredients:

1 marshmallow (regular size)

1 sheet of honey graham cracker, halved crosswise into 2 squares

1 1/2 teaspoons of sweetened coconut chips

One 0.375-ounce square milk chocolate

1/2 teaspoon of peanut butter

1/4 teaspoon of caramel sauce

Directions:

Start by preheating your air fryer to 400 degrees F or 204 degrees C, and set it aside. Place the marshmallow in the air fryer for approximately 3 minutes until it's toasted to your liking.

Lay the graham cracker squares flat on a plate, with the hole side facing down.

On one graham square, sprinkle sweetened coconut chips, followed by placing the square of milk chocolate on top.

Spread the peanut butter evenly on the other plain graham square.

After 2 minutes, put both graham squares inside the air fryer.

Roll the toasted marshmallow onto the graham square with peanut butter and air fry them together for an additional minute.

Carefully transfer the graham squares onto a plate using a spatula, ensuring no chocolate chips are left behind.

Add a drizzle of caramel sauce to the graham square with chocolate and coconut chips.

Quickly sandwich the two graham squares together while the s'more is still warm and gooey.

Nutrition Facts:

Servings: 2

Amount per serving:

Calories: 71

Total Fat: 1.4g (2% Daily Value)

Saturated Fat: 0.3g (1% Daily Value)

Cholesterol: 0mg (0% Daily Value)

Sodium: 52mg (2% Daily Value)

Total Carbohydrate: 6.6g (2% Daily Value)

Dietary Fiber: 0.3g (1% Daily Value)

Total Sugars: 2.5g

Protein: 0.8g

Baked Walleye

Preparation Time: 15 Minutes | **Cook Time:** 25 Minutes | **Servings:** 2

Ingredients:

1 pound Walleye Fillets

1/2 cup chopped Onion

1 tablespoon olive oil

1/2 teaspoon salt

1/4 teaspoon Morton's Seasoning Blend

Directions:

Begin by preheating your air fryer to 400 degrees F or 204 degrees C.

Take a standard-sized baking sheet and cut a piece of foil that is double the size of the sheet pan.

Place half of the foil on the sheet pan, ensuring that the shiny side is facing down and the dull side is up. This will allow you to fold the other half of the foil over the fish to create a seal while cooking.

Spread the olive oil evenly on the foil covering the sheet pan.

Sprinkle a pinch of seasoned salt and pepper onto the oiled foil.

Lay the Walleye fillets in a single layer on top of the seasoned oil, making sure you do this on the sheet pan.

Lightly season the fish fillets one more time with a dash of salt and pepper.

Slice the onion into thin rings, separate them, and place them on top of the Walleye fillets.

Fold the foil over the fish, completely covering it.

Roll the foil ends together, starting with the opposite side of the folded foil. Then, roll both ends to seal the fish into a foil pouch. Be cautious not to puncture the bottom of the foil.

Using a sharp knife, gently poke a few holes into the top of the foil pouch, ensuring not to pierce the bottom.

Bake the fish in the preheated air fryer for 25 minutes.

Once done, carefully open the foil pouch and serve.

Nutrition Facts:

Servings: 2

Amount per serving:

Calories: 568

Total Fat: 13.1g (17% Daily Value)

Saturated Fat: 1g (5% Daily Value)

Cholesterol: 263mg (88% Daily Value)

Sodium: 306mg (13% Daily Value)

Total Carbohydrate: 5.1g (2% Daily Value)

Dietary Fiber: 1.2g (4% Daily Value)

Total Sugars: 2.3g

Protein: 105.9g

Vegan Air Fryer Taquitos

Prep: 15 Minutes | **Cook Time:** 35-40 Minutes | **Makes:** 2 Servings

Ingredients:

1 large russet potato, peeled

1 teaspoon of plant-based butter

2 tablespoons of diced onions

1 clove garlic, minced

1/4 cup of plant-based butter

2 tablespoons of unsweetened, plain almond milk

Salt and ground black pepper to taste

6 corn tortillas

Avocado oil cooking spray

Directions:

Begin by placing the peeled russet potato into a saucepan and covering it with salted water. Bring the water to a boil, then reduce the heat to medium-low and simmer until the potato is tender, which should take about 20 minutes.

While the potato is boiling, melt 1 teaspoon of plant-based butter in a skillet. Saute the diced onions in the skillet until they become soft and translucent, which typically takes 3 to 5 minutes. Add the minced garlic and continue cooking until it becomes fragrant, about 1 more minute. Set this mixture aside.

Once the potato is cooked, drain it and transfer it to a bowl. Add 1/4 cup of plant-based butter and the unsweetened almond milk to the bowl. Season the mixture with salt and ground black pepper to taste. Mash the potato and mix in the sauteed onion and garlic until well combined.

Heat the corn tortillas in a skillet or directly on the grates of a gas stove until they become soft and pliable.

Place 3 tablespoons of the potato mixture down the center of each tortilla, then fold them over and roll them up to form taquitos.

Preheat an air fryer to 400 degrees F or 204 degrees C.

Place the taquitos in the air fryer basket, ensuring they are not touching each other, and lightly mist them with avocado oil cooking spray. Cook in batches if necessary.

Air fry the taquitos until they become golden brown and crispy, which should take approximately 6 to 9 minutes. Turn the taquitos over, mist them with more avocado oil, and continue air frying for an additional 3 to 5 minutes, or until they are thoroughly cooked and crispy.

Nutrition Facts:

   Servings: 2

   Amount per serving:

   Calories: 584

   Total Fat: 13.4g (17% Daily Value)

   Saturated Fat: 3.6g (18% Daily Value)

   Cholesterol: 0mg (0% Daily Value)

   Sodium: 46mg (2% Daily Value)

   Total Carbohydrate: 66.6g (24% Daily Value)

   Dietary Fiber: 9.2g (33% Daily Value)

   Total Sugars: 3g

   Protein: 18.7g

Air Fryer Turkey Fajitas

Preparation Time: 15 Minutes | **Cook Time:** 25-30 Minutes | **Servings:** 2

Ingredients:

1 tablespoon of chili powder

1 tablespoon of ground cumin

½ tablespoon of paprika

½ tablespoon of dried Mexican oregano

1 teaspoon of freshly ground black pepper

1 teaspoon of garlic powder

½ teaspoon of onion powder

2 limes, divided

1-pound skinless, boneless turkey breast, cut into 1/2-inch-thick slices

1 ½ tablespoons of vegetable oil, divided

1 large red bell pepper, sliced into strips

1 medium yellow bell pepper, sliced into strips

1 large red onion, halved and sliced into strips

1 jalapeno pepper, seeded and chopped, or more to taste

¼ cup chopped fresh cilantro

Directions:

In a small bowl, combine chili powder, ground cumin, paprika, dried Mexican oregano, black pepper, garlic powder, and onion powder.

Squeeze the juice of 1 lime over the turkey breast slices. Sprinkle the seasoning mixture over the meat, and add 1 tablespoon of vegetable oil. Toss to coat and set aside.

Place the sliced bell peppers and onion in a bowl, and drizzle with the remaining vegetable oil. Toss to coat.

Preheat an air fryer to 400 degrees F or 204 degrees C, following the manufacturer's instructions.

Cook the bell peppers and onions in the preheated air fryer for 8 minutes. Shake the basket and continue cooking for another 5 minutes.

Add the chopped jalapeno pepper and cook for an additional 5 minutes.

Open the air fryer basket, shake to distribute the mixture, and place the turkey strips in a single layer on top of the vegetables. Close the basket and cook for 7 to 8 minutes.

Open the basket again, shake to distribute the mixture once more, and continue cooking until the turkey strips are slightly crispy and no longer pink in the centers, and the peppers are tender, about 5 more minutes.

Remove the basket and transfer the fajita mixture to a bowl or platter. Top with chopped cilantro and squeeze the juice of the remaining lime over the fajitas.

Nutrition Facts:

Servings: 2

Amount per serving:

Calories: 373

Total Fat: 10g (13% Daily Value)

Saturated Fat: 3.3g (16% Daily Value)

Cholesterol: 132mg (44% Daily Value)

Sodium: 130mg (6% Daily Value)

Total Carbohydrate: 18.8g (7% Daily Value)

Dietary Fiber: 5.6g (20% Daily Value)

Total Sugars: 7.3g

Protein: 53.8g

Air Fryer Tacos de Papa

Prep: 15 Minutes | **Cook Time:** 5-15 Minutes | **Makes:** 2 Servings

Ingredients:

1 cup of water

1 (4 ounces) package instant mashed potatoes

1/2 cup shredded Cheddar cheese

1 green onion, chopped

1/2 teaspoon ground cumin

10 corn tortillas

Non-stick cooking spray

1/2 cup salsa verde

1/4 cup crumbled cotija cheese

Directions:

Heat water in a medium saucepan until it comes to a boil.

Remove the saucepan from the heat and stir in the instant mashed potatoes. Use a fork to thoroughly moisten all the potatoes, and let it stand for 5 minutes. Stir in the shredded Cheddar cheese, chopped green onion, and ground cumin.

Preheat your air fryer to 400 degrees F (204 degrees C).

Wrap the corn tortillas in a damp paper towel and microwave them on high for approximately 20 seconds, or until they become warm.

Spread 1 tablespoon of the potato mixture in the center of each tortilla and fold them over to create tacos. Repeat this step with the remaining tortillas.

Place the tacos in the air fryer basket in batches. Spray the tops of the tacos with non-stick cooking spray.

Cook the tacos in the air fryer until they become crispy, which should take about 5 minutes. Transfer them to a serving platter and repeat the process to cook the remaining tacos.

Drizzle the salsa verde over the tacos and generously sprinkle them with crumbled cotija cheese.

Nutrition Facts:

Servings: 2

Amount per serving:

Calories: 596

Total Fat: 13.3g (17% Daily Value)

Saturated Fat: 6.6g (33% Daily Value)

Cholesterol: 30mg (10% Daily Value)

Sodium: 642mg (28% Daily Value)

Total Carbohydrate: 103.3g (38% Daily Value)

Dietary Fiber: 11.8g (42% Daily Value)

Total Sugars: 4.2g

Protein: 19.6g

Air Fryer Shrimp "Boil"

Preparation Time: 15 Minutes | **Cook Time:** 20-25 Minutes | **Servings:** 2

Ingredients:

1 pound baby red potatoes

1/4 cup of water

8 ounces Cajun-style andouille sausage, sliced

1 ear of corn, sliced in half lengthwise and cut into 2-inch pieces

1 medium onion, sliced into petals

4 tablespoons of olive oil, divided

3 teaspoons of seafood seasoning, divided

1 pound of large raw shrimp, peeled and deveined

1 lemon, cut into wedges

Directions:

Preheat your air fryer to 400 degrees F (204 degrees C).

Begin by placing the baby red potatoes in a microwave-safe bowl. Add 1/4 cup of water and microwave on high for 5 minutes.

Once microwaved, cool the potatoes by running the bowl under cold water until they are cool enough to touch. Slice the potatoes in half lengthwise and place them in a large bowl.

Add the sliced andouille sausage, corn pieces, and onion petals to the bowl with the potatoes. Mix in 3 tablespoons of olive oil and 2 teaspoons of seafood seasoning, stirring to coat all the ingredients evenly.

In a separate bowl, place the large raw shrimp and add the remaining 1 tablespoon of olive oil and 1 teaspoon of seafood seasoning. Stir to coat the shrimp evenly.

Transfer 1/2 of the potato mixture into the basket of the air fryer and cook for 10 minutes. Stir the mixture and continue to cook for an additional 5 minutes.

Add 1/2 of the seasoned shrimp to the air fryer and cook until the potatoes are tender, the sausage is cooked through, the shrimp are bright pink on the outside, and the meat is opaque, which should take about 5 more minutes.

Transfer the cooked mixture to a serving plate and repeat the cooking process with the remaining potato mixture and shrimp.

Serve the Cajun-inspired dish with lemon wedges for added zest and flavor.

Nutrition Facts:

Servings: 2

Amount per serving:

Calories: 1026

Total Fat: 61.4g (79% Daily Value)

Saturated Fat: 14.6g (73% Daily Value)

Cholesterol: 419mg (140% Daily Value)

Sodium: 1170mg (51% Daily Value)

Total Carbohydrate: 51.9g (19% Daily Value)

Dietary Fiber: 9g (32% Daily Value)

Total Sugars: 4.8g

Protein: 73.5g

Air Fried Fish Sinigang sa Miso
Preparation Time: 15 Minutes | **Cook Time:** 15-20 Minutes | **Servings:** 2

Ingredients:

1 piece of cleaned tilapia

40 grams of Knorr Sinigang sa Sampaloc Recipe mix

1/4 cup of miso

1 bunch of mustard leaves

8 pieces of okra

1 piece of yellow onion, wedged

6 ounces of daikon radish, sliced

2 pieces of tomato, wedged

4 pieces of long green chili

6 to 8 cups of water

1/2 teaspoon of ground black pepper

1 1/2 teaspoons of cooking oil

1 teaspoon of salt

Fish sauce to taste

Directions:

Create slits on both sides of the tilapia. Rub salt all over the fish, followed by rubbing with cooking oil.

Use an air fryer to cook the fish. Air fry each side at 400 degrees F or 204 degrees C for 10 minutes. Remove the cooked fish and let it cool down.

In a cooking pot, pour in the water and bring it to a boil.

Add the onion, tomato, daikon radish, and miso to the boiling water. Let it re-boil.

Place the cooked tilapia into the pot and let it cook for an additional 2 minutes after the water re-boils. Add the Knorr Sinigang Recipe Mix and stir.

Add the okra and long green peppers to the pot. Cover and cook over medium heat for 5 minutes.

Finally, add the mustard leaves and season with fish sauce and ground black pepper. Cover and cook for an additional 3 minutes.

Transfer the flavorful tilapia Sinigang and Miso broth to a serving bowl. Serve hot and enjoy!

Nutrition Facts:

Servings: 2

Amount per serving:

Calories: 36

Total Fat: 3.5g (4% Daily Value)

Saturated Fat: 0.5g (3% Daily Value)

Cholesterol: 2mg (1% Daily Value)

Sodium: 23mg (1% Daily Value)

Total Carbohydrate: 0.6g (0% Daily Value)

Dietary Fiber: 0.3g (1% Daily Value)

Total Sugars: 0.1g

Protein: 0.8g

Air Fryer Rack of Lamb with Roasted Garlic Aioli

Preparation Time: 15 Minutes | **Cook Time:** 22 Minutes | **Servings:** 2

Ingredients:

One 8-rib rack of lamb, frenched (1 1/4 to 1 1/2 pounds)

3 tablespoons of extra-virgin olive oil

Kosher salt and freshly ground black pepper

1/2 cup of grated Parmesan

1/3 cup of Panko breadcrumbs

1 large clove garlic, grated

1 teaspoon of finely chopped fresh thyme

1 teaspoon of finely chopped fresh rosemary

Non-stick cooking spray, for the air-fryer basket and lamb

Aioli:

6 large cloves garlic (unpeeled)

2 tablespoons of olive oil

1/2 cup of mayonnaise

1 teaspoon of lemon zest plus 2 teaspoons fresh lemon juice

1 1/2 teaspoons of Worcestershire sauce

Kosher salt and freshly ground black pepper

Directions:

1. Begin by rubbing both sides of the rack of lamb with 1 tablespoon of olive oil, then season it with 2 teaspoons of salt and a generous amount of freshly ground black pepper. Set it aside on a large plate.
2. In a large shallow bowl or pie plate, combine the grated Parmesan, Panko breadcrumbs, remaining 2 tablespoons of olive oil, grated garlic, thyme, and rosemary. Press the Parmesan mixture firmly onto the lamb to create an even layer.
3. For the aioli: Place the unpeeled garlic cloves on a piece of aluminum foil, add the olive oil, a pinch of salt, and a few grinds of pepper. Fold the foil sides upwards to create a sealed pouch.
4. Preheat an air fryer to 400 degrees F or 204 degrees C. Spray the air-fryer basket with cooking spray. Place the lamb, fat side up, and the garlic pouch into the basket. Spray the top of the lamb with cooking spray.
5. Air-fry the lamb until the crust is crisp and deep golden brown and the meat reaches your desired doneness. Approximately 18 minutes for medium-rare, 20 minutes for

medium, and 22 minutes for medium-well. (The garlic can cook for the same duration as the lamb.)

6. Transfer the cooked lamb to a cutting board, cover it loosely with foil, and let it rest for 10 minutes. Meanwhile, carefully open the foil packet containing the garlic. Squeeze out the tender garlic cloves into a medium bowl and mash them with the olive oil from the pouch until smooth. Mix in the mayonnaise, lemon zest and juice, and Worcestershire sauce until well combined. Season the aioli with salt and pepper to taste. Set it aside.

7. Once the lamb has rested, slice it between the bones into individual chops. Serve the lamb chops warm, accompanied by the aioli.

Nutrition Facts:

Servings: 2

Amount per serving:

Calories: 891

Total Fat: 73.1g (94% Daily Value)

Saturated Fat: 21.7g (109% Daily Value)

Cholesterol: 120mg (40% Daily Value)

Sodium: 1364mg (59% Daily Value)

Total Carbohydrate: 27.4g (10% Daily Value)

Dietary Fiber: 1g (4% Daily Value)

Total Sugars: 6.3g

Protein: 37.6g

APPENDIX: RECIPE INDEX

Made in the USA
Las Vegas, NV
08 June 2024

90894448R10090